the dwarves, who had long served as the King's Own Guard, decided to take the kingdom from their human masters. YOU are thrust into the action as Galen, a young person whose family is the first to be captured by the dwarven troops. You escape and set out to warn the prince and to rescue your parents. It is up to you to pick your own path into ADVENTURE.

What will you do?

You have narrowly escaped capture by the dwarves. The sounds of their hunt still surround you. But you must make a choice:

1) Fight the dwarves and try to rescue your parents; turn to page 143.

2) Hide and hope they don't find you; turn to page 31.

3) Try to escape their clutches by making a run for it; turn to page 59.

Whichever path you pick, you are sure to find adventure, as you turn the pages of

REVOLT OF THE DWARVES

An ENDLESS QUEST™ Book #5

REVOLT of the DWARVES

Cover Art by Larry Elmore
Interior Art by Jim Holloway

TSR Hobbies, Inc.

This book is for John Blanton,
who is very special.

Also by Rose Estes and published by TSR Hobbies, Inc.:

DUNGEON OF DREAD
MOUNTAIN OF MIRRORS
PILLARS OF PENTEGARN
RETURN TO BROOKMERE
REVENGE OF THE RAINBOW DRAGONS

Distributed to the book trade in the United States by Random House, Inc. and in Canada by Random House of Canada, Ltd.
Distributed in the United Kingdom by TSR (UK) Ltd.
Distributed to the toy and hobby trade by regional distributors.

First Printing: January, 1983 Second Printing — April 1983
Printed in the United States of America
Library of Congress Catalog Card Number: 82-51205
ISBN 0-88038-020-9

9 8 7 6 5 4 3 2

TSR Hobbies, Inc.
POB 756
Lake Geneva, WI 53147

TSR Hobbies (UK) Ltd.
The Mill, Rathmore Road
Cambridge CB1 4AD
United Kingdom

ook, Dad! What's that dark cloud over there? It's not the storm, is it?"

Looking over the backs of the four horses that pull your cart, your father squints, then says, "Riders. Lots of them and coming fast."

"Are they bandits, Paul?" asks your mother fearfully, clutching her shawl to her throat.

"No, Martha. They can't be bandits. The Dwarven Guard cleaned up the last of them ten years ago. I don't know who they are, but the way they're riding we'll soon find out.

"Galen, grab that puppy of yours and get under cover in that pile of bedclothes."

"But I want to stay here. If there's trouble, I can help, too."

"Do as your father says," snaps your mother. "And don't come out till we say it's safe."

You know better than to argue with your mother, so you get off the narrow wooden seat and wriggle through the crowded cart.

"Well, no one said I couldn't watch," you whisper to Woofy, who licks your face in reply.

Snuggling down into the pile of blankets, you quiet the puppy, who thinks you're trying to play. Then you arrange the blankets so that you can see.

Soon, a faint rumble becomes the drumming thunder of horses' hoofs.

"Hold your team!" demands a harsh voice.

"Oh, Paul! It's the Guard!" cries your mother. "Thank heavens, we're safe."

Pulling the team to a complete stop, your

father calls, "Ho! Guard! What is your business with us? We are anxious to camp before the storm breaks. Speak, and let us be on our way."

"Do you dare to speak so to the King's Guard?" snarls a menacing voice.

"Teach the humans to be polite!" urges another of the uniformed dwarves.

Your mother clings to your father's arm.

Rain begins to fall. All around you are the sounds of horses. Saddle leather creaks beneath the weight of the armored Dwarven Guard, and you feel the presence of unseen riders closing in.

"Now, now, lads. Is this any way to speak to those we have vowed to protect?" asks a honeyed voice. "Come, let us not be hasty. Let's find out how the situation lies. After all, lads, we wouldn't want to make a mistake now, would we?"

There is a long moment of silence. Then a few voices mutter, "Sneed's right."

"Well, then. Here we all are. Nice and pleasant," says Sneed. "Surely all a mistake. But these are lads with quick tempers, so please humor us by answering a few questions."

"I'm sure we've done no wrong," says your mother. "What do you want to know?"

"Just a few questions," says Sneed. "Like where you've been and where you're going."

"Why, Captain, we're going to the prince's coronation, of course. And as to where we've been, we've been mapping. My husband is the royal mapmaker."

"Royal mapmaker, eh? Splendid occupation. So useful. And are you traveling alone?"

Your father answers quickly, "Yes, Captain, quite alone. Just me and the missus."

"All by yourselves. Splendid, just splendid," Sneed beams. "You see, lads, what comes of talking first? Now we know who these fine people are. Avoid mistakes, I always say. Now we know they are alone. Seize them!"

Before your father can protest, heavy hands pull him and your mother from the cart. Your mother screams and your father curses, but rough laughter drowns out their cries.

"You see, lads. It is as I told you. Who would suspect the king's own Dwarven Guard of treachery? No one, until it's far too late. Soon, all that is owed to us for long years of protecting humans will be ours. Now, tie these two up. We'll take them back to the caves. A mapmaker will be useful to our new kingdom.

"Soon we will launch our attack. With the prince in our hands, the kingdom is ours!

"Drive the wagon into the rocks and search it for gold and maps. Then burn it!"

Hidden in the wagon, you hear Sneed's order and know that you have three choices:

1) Fight the dwarves and try to rescue your parents; turn to page 143.

2) Hide and hope they don't find you; turn to page 31.

3) Try to escape; turn to page 59.

"Do you have anything valuable on you?" you ask the old king.

"Just this," answers Hume, pulling a gold chain from around his neck. Dangling at the end of the chain is a brilliant black fire opal the size of an egg.

"Let me have it for just a minute," you say.

The old dwarf hesitates and then hands you the necklace.

You wait nervously until the guard turns his head away from you. Then you duck down and place the necklace on the ground at the corner of the corridor. Handing Woofy to Hume, you pick up a large, loose rock and wait. Soon, a gasp of surprise tells you that the dwarf has seen the gem. Footsteps draw near. You raise the rock high . . .

Please turn to page 103.

Confusion sets in and you are unable to actually make a decision. The snake's musky scent fills your nostrils and you begin to grow very, very sleepy.

Your last thought is that if luck is with you, Sandy will rescue you. If not, you've done the best you could. You know that your parents would be proud of you. With that, you surrender yourself to fate and let the blackness take you.

THE END

"We shouldn't take chances like this," you say angrily. "I don't want to get eaten by a spider. I'm going to sleep outside!"

Whimsy snuggles up on one of the soft beds, twists a long blond curl around her finger, and says, "You do whatever you think best, Galen. I'm going to stay here in a nice soft bed."

You would like to change your mind, but you don't know how to do so without appearing silly. You stomp up the passage, smash the trap door aside, and walk into a dark, dismal night.

You crouch fearfully under the shelter of a large pine tree. Before long, rain begins to fall and water drips down upon you. Unseen animals roar around you and you huddle in fear of your life. You wish you could go back down the tunnel, but you are afraid Whimsy will laugh at you. So you do not move.

Finally, morning arrives. Rainbow prisms of pure color fill the forest, but you are unable to appreciate its beauty because you are cold, wet, tired, and cranky.

It does not help when Whimsy, bright-eyed and beautiful, pushes back the trap door, stretches, and says, "Good morning, Galen. Did you have a nice night? I did! Isn't it a glorious morning? Are you ready to go?"

You snarl in answer and the three of you start off once more.

Please turn to page 94.

At last the water calms and, using what little strength remains, you climb astride the log. No sooner have you done so than you see a head bobbing in the water. Sandy!

Quickly you paddle the log over to the drifting figure and with great difficulty pull him up onto the log.

"Thank the gods, Sandy! I thought you were dead," you exclaim as he rolls over weakly and spits water from his mouth.

"I feel dead, or at least drowned. I must have swallowed half the river," splutters Sandy as he shakes water from his hair.

"But we are alive, Sandy. That's what counts. I really think we'll be all right now. We escaped the monster, and I think I can see the top of the city's towers above the trees. All we have to do now is get through that swamp ahead and we'll be fine. You'll see-e-e-ee!"

A band of steel closes about your ankle and you are jerked off the log and under the surface of the murky water. You struggle to free yourself, but you cannot. Just when you think your lungs will burst, something grabs your hair and yanks you out of the water.

Water blurs your vision. You rub your eyes to clear them and then wish you had not.

Two greenish-brown eyes peer at you. A long snout covered with thick, armorlike green scales and filled with sharp pointy teeth gapes inches from your face.

Behind you, Sandy screams with terror. He too has been seized.

"What you do in Squamata's swamp?" hisses the frightening creature.

"I didn't know it was anyone's swamp," you stutter. "We don't really even want to be here. We're trying to get to the city."

"Why you not use road like other peoples? Why you come to swamp? You must be dwarves. You must be enemy come to kill Squamata and lizardmen. But you fail. Now you die!"

The awful mouth opens and the reek of rotten fish rolls over you.

"No! No!" you yell, struggling against the iron grip. "You've got it all wrong. We're not dwarves. And we can't go by the road. The dwarves are lying in wait trying to kill me!"

You are lowered with a splash. The toothy mouth closes and an amber eye squints thoughtfully at you.

"Why dwarves try to kill you? Dwarves enemies of lizardmen. But dwarves work for king. Dwarves like peoples."

"No, they don't. These dwarves just pretend to." And quickly you tell the tale.

Squamata listens carefully and then grunting, hissing, and clicking in a strange lizard language, speaks to his followers. With no warning, you and Sandy are lifted and placed firmly upon the backs of two seven-foot-tall lizardmen. They turn and swim into the murky gloom of the swamp. Soon you are lost.

At last the lizardmen slither, one after another, onto a muddy bank crowded with crude huts. Almost instantly, you are surrounded by hundreds of the scaly creatures who look at you with hatred and hunger. You and Sandy and Woofy huddle together in fear.

Squamata moves through the crowd, crouches down, and pokes you with a large, clawed hand. "Tell story to all," he grunts. "Then we decide if truth, or if we eat you. Maybe we eat you anyhow if no one care."

Once again you tell the story, making it as interesting as possible. Once more the lizardmen speak together in their own tongue.

Finally, Squamata turns to you and says slowly, "Lizardmen hate dwarves. Dwarves kill lizardmen for sport. Dwarves make fine weapons. Lizardmen want weapons. Dwarves laugh and say no. Squamata go to city with you. Help warn prince. Kill dwarves. Prince happy. Prince give lizardmen weapons. You say yes and lizardmen help you. You say no and lizardmen eat you. You choose."

1) If you decide to trust the lizardmen, turn to page 98.

2) If you decide you do not trust the lizardmen, run to the swamp and try to escape. Turn to page 25.

Gathering your courage you step up to the guard nearest you and tug on the leg of his uniform. "Excuse me, sir," you say. "I must see the prince at once. It's extremely important. It's a matter of life and death."

Cold blue eyes stare down at you over a huge handlebar mustache. "Remove your hand from my uniform at once, you grubby pixie. What are you doing here? Do you have an appointment? No one sees the prince without an appointment. For that matter, no pixies are allowed in the city. Now, remove yourself and your dirty dog from the steps, immediately!"

You feel the cold eyes on your back as you reluctantly go back down the steps.

Please return to page 145
and make another choice.

"I don't really think I can help you," you tell the old dwarf.

At your words his shoulders sag, and he seems to age before your very eyes.

"No, I suppose it was too much to hope for," sighs the dwarf. "Well, come with me. I will show you where your parents are."

You follow the bent form to a cell in a nearby tunnel. The door is heavily barred, but the dwarf helps you, and soon the door creaks open. Your parents hurry out.

"Oh, Galen," cries your mother, flinging her arms around you. "I thought you were dead. I thought we'd never see you again."

"Now, Martha," says your father gruffly, "don't smother the child." Yet when your mother loosens her hold, your father squeezes your arm hard and there are tears in his eyes.

"No time for reunions," grumbles the dwarf. "Time for that later . . . if you live."

You follow him closely as he shuffles through the corridors. Soon you reach an unguarded exit and escape into the night.

You and your parents hide in the hills. In the morning you watch the mounted dwarven army ride out. As evening's shadows lengthen on the mountains, the army returns, victorious.

Over the years you and your parents live under the grim rule of the evil monarch Sneed the Supreme. You often wonder what would have happened if you had helped the dwarf.

THE END

Using your poles, you steer for the island and crash into its point. The current pulls at the raft and you have to fight to drag it up on the rocky shore.

Tucking Woofy inside your shirt, you begin climbing the shiny green rock. Soon the two of you stand at the top of the small island. To your left the river plunges straight down and disappears in a cloud of white spray. To your right, the water falls down the boulders in ladderlike steps.

Suddenly, the island lurches to the left. You and Sandy fall to the ground and clutch at a rocky ridge that runs down the center. A deep roar splits the air. The ground shakes beneath you. Two black eyes glare at you and a sharp beak clacks open and shut.

Somehow, you and Sandy make your way back to the raft just as it slips into the river.

"Quick, Sandy, jump for it!"

Angry black eyes and a fearful beak loom over you. The monster opens its mouth and reaches for you.

"It's going to grab us," screams Sandy.

1) If you want to go down the waterfall on the raft, turn to page 147.

2) If you want to try to go down the giant steps, turn to page 84.

3) If you want to try to talk to the monster, turn to page 48.

"I don't know, Woofy. Maybe I had better try to reach the city. I certainly don't want to go after those dwarves. I'm scared of them, and even if I did, I doubt if I'd be able to rescue my folks. I'd probably just wind up getting caught myself. And just heading out trying to find a grown-up sounds kind of chancy. Even if I found grown-ups somewhere in this wilderness, how do I know they would help? It's such a weird story, probably no one would believe me."

"I believe you and I'm a grown-up," says a tiny voice behind you.

"Who's that? Who's there?" you cry in alarm. A brilliant white light, much too bright to look at, appears in front of you. You shield your eyes, and the light dims to a soft glow.

In the middle of the glow stands a small winged figure only slightly taller than Woofy, and it's unlike anything you've ever seen before.

"Didn't your mother ever tell you it's not polite to stare? Anyhow, I'll repeat—I'm an adult and I believe you."

"But you're a . . . you're a . . ." you stammer, floundering helplessly.

"I'm a pixie, dummy, a pixie!"

"But you don't really exist. My dad says so. Dad says I let my imagination run away with me. Maybe I'm only dreaming. Go away. You're not real."

"It would serve you right if I did go away," says the small creature angrily. "But it

wouldn't be fair. You don't stand a chance without me."

Heaving a great sigh, the pixie says, "That's the problem with you humans. You keep ignoring your imagination. You should trust it more often. Leave your mind open and you'll be able to believe in glorious creatures like me."

"Are you really a pixie?" you ask in amazement. "And a grown-up one, too?"

"Sure. I'm just like any other woman, except I'm twice as beautiful, twice as smart, and I can do lots of magic stuff. And, of course, I'm a lot smaller, not all large and clumsy like you humans. Don't you think I'm pretty?"

Masses of blond, curling ringlets frame the tiny, delicate, heart-shaped face. Large violet eyes fringed with thick, dark lashes look up at you mischievously. A dimple lurks at the corner of a pink rosebud mouth, and shimmering, gauzy wings fan the air delicately. Garments that seem to be made of silken rainbows cover the enchanting creature.

Swallowing hard, you say, "I think you're the prettiest thing I've ever seen."

Settling a tiny crown of lily-of-the-valley flowers on her head, she fluffs her shining curls and says, "Well, I knew that all the time. But it's always nice to hear it. You know, you're pretty smart—for a human, that is."

The pixie stares at you for a minute as though trying to make up her mind about something. Finally she says, "Woofy has been telling me about your problems. I suppose I could help you for a little while. Things have been pretty dull around here lately. And I don't like dwarves at all. They pull the wings off pixies and sprites every chance they get! Can you imagine?" The pixie's voice shakes with anger. "So, Galen, if I can help you show those nasty dwarves a thing or two, and as long as it's fun, I'll help you."

"How do you know my name?" you stammer.

"Try not to be dim, dear. Woofy told me, of course. We had a nice long chat while you were sleeping. It's mostly because of him that I've decided to help. Animals always get hurt in your stupid human wars. And why should they? Animals never have wars. It really makes me angry!" The pixie stamps her foot in midair.

"But who are you?"

"Oh, yes, I guess I should introduce myself. My full name is Whimsicality P. Delphinium, but you can call me Whimsy."

"Whimsy—what a grand name!"

"Yes, it is, isn't it."

"But how can you help?"

"Simple! I know the forest like my own living room, which I suppose it is. I'll just take you straight through the forest to the king of the pixies. He'll know what to do."

"Great! Let's go." You drop to the ground and begin to wriggle out from under the rock. The opening is very narrow. Only by pressing yourself flat in the mud are you able to squeeze through. You carefully look around for dwarves before you stand up. Last night's mud still clings to your clothes and hair. New mud covers you from head to toe.

"Ugh! I don't know if I want to be seen with you. It's not bad enough that you're a human, but a dirty human is too much to bear!"

The pixie hovers in midair before you, a disapproving frown on her face. She has flung a cape of brilliant red cardinal feathers over her shoulders and as she shimmers in the sunlight you feel large, drab, and clumsy.

"I'm sorry. I can't do anything about my size or my appearance," you say regretfully.

"But I can," says Whimsy. "We'll go to my friend the dryad. She's got a shrinking potion that she's been saving. I'll have her let you drink it, and then I'll get you some spare pixie clothes."

"Shrink me?" you cry in fear. "Will it hurt? Will I stay small forever?"

"Don't be silly," says Whimsy, and without even looking to see if you are following, she flies down the hill.

1) If you choose to go with the pixie and take your chances on being shrunk, turn to page 92.

2) If you choose to leave the pixie and go after the dwarves instead, thank Whimsy for her offer of help and turn to page 34.

"Quick!" whispers Sandy. "Help me get two of these poles loose."

You kneel on the rough boards and pry the poles loose from their water-soaked ties.

More quickly than you would wish, the black bulk of the dragon looms before you.

"Try to go right smack between those two big rocks. Maybe he won't even wake up."

The brown waters wash against the black rock, forming a wave of tan foam. The rock on your left is smooth and covered with green moss. Your pole strikes and then slides off its slippery surface. The raft drifts closer and closer. Soon it will bump against the rock and perhaps wake the dragon up.

"Quick! Try again," you hiss, and the two poles wedge against the slimy rock.

Fear lends you strength, and the poles bite deep into the moss. Relief floods over you as you feel solid rock beneath your pole. The dark bulk of the dragon passes over you. Steadily you push away, and soon the dragon falls behind.

You collapse weakly on the raft, happy that you have escaped. Suddenly, Woofy begins to bark excitedly. You quickly grab his muzzle.

"Did it hear?" Sandy asks in horror.

You stare back at the dragon. For one moment, you think you see a silver eye staring at you. But maybe you're mistaken. Might it be the sun glinting off the water?

Please turn to page 41.

"Sandy, I don't trust them," you whisper. "When I give the signal, run for the swamp. We'll have to try to escape and get to the city ourselves."

"Um, Galen, do you really think this is a smart thing to do?"

"Trust me, Sandy, trust me. Lizardmen are closely related to snakes and reptiles. Would you trust a snake? I mean, how do we know they'll keep their word? Trust me, Sandy. NOW RUN!"

Squamata watches as the two of you rush toward the tangled swamp. Heaving a great sigh, he shakes his scaly head. "Peoples dumb. Dwarves dumb. Lizardmen say 'help,' peoples run away. Lizardmen not worry. Peoples and dwarves kill each other and lizardmen win in the end."

"Catch peoples?" grunts a large lizard.

"No, not bother," answers Squamata. "Peoples not find way out of swamp. Too bad for them now."

Grunting and hissing in agreement, the lizardmen stretch out in the warm sun on the muddy bank. One by one they close their amber eyes and sleep.

Somewhere in the depths of the swamp you look around in fear and confusion and wonder if this is . . .

THE END

"Thank you very much, but I think I should stay with Whimsy," you say nervously.

The dryad does not speak, but the air is charged with electricity. "I should have known you would not have the courage. Few humans do. Very well, then. Drink the potion and go with Whimsy. But don't come back whining if you don't like what happens to you."

Angrily, she snatches a flower, pours a white, milky liquid into its cupped petals, and thrusts it at you.

Not wanting to admit you are afraid, you quickly swallow the thick fluid. An icy, shivery tingle covers your body. You struggle under a heavy, clinging weight. Suddenly you realize you are being smothered by your own clothes!

"Great!" says Whimsy. "You're just right."

You realize with a shock that you and Whimsy are now exactly the same size!

"I'm shrunk. I'm really shrunk!" you cry, excitedly examining your new and tiny self.

"Oh, stop carrying on. That's what we came here for. You should be happy that it worked. Here, put these on. They're second-hand, but they'll do unless you want to go around looking like that," she says with a giggle.

You snatch the clothes and change quickly inside the gigantic folds of your own clothing.

"Wow, Galen, you really look good!"

"How come I keep changing colors?"

"Because all pixie clothes are woven out of spider silk. It's almost as good as chameleon

skin. But these are only second best. We hide extra clothes in different places around the forest for emergencies."

Whimsy turns to the tree spirit. "Thank you very much for your help, dryad."

"Goodbye," whispers the creature, and she dissolves to mist and fades into her tree.

"Does she always come and go like that?"

"No. We were lucky. It's very hard to find her if she doesn't want to be found."

"Well, what about being small? Am I going to have to stay this way forever?"

"I'm not sure," says the pixie. "I've never shrunk a human before. Besides, what's wrong with being this size? I think it's just grand!"

"Never mind," you say with a sigh. "But now that I'm the right size, we'd better go."

"Okay, climb on behind me. We're light enough for Woofy to carry both of us." She flies up to his back and looks down at you.

You try to jump up but do not succeed. "Down, Woofy! Lie down!" you command.

Woofy turns around and licks you from head to toe, knocking you down. Whimsy giggles and nearly falls off the dog's back.

"Oh, if you could only see how silly you look," she laughs. "Your face is all red."

You are so angry you rise and stomp away.

"Oh, Galen, come back. I'm sorry. Really I am. I didn't mean to hurt your feelings. Don't be angry. I'll be good. Come get up here."

But you walk into the dark without a word. Far in the distance you see the bright red twinkling of a campfire. The smell of roasting meat hangs in the air. You begin to run.

"Wait! Where are you going?" calls Whimsy.

"Over there. I'm tired, I'm hungry, and I'm cold. Maybe whoever made that fire will share their dinner with me. I don't like you anymore. You laugh at me and tease me. So just go away. I don't need you anymore!"

"Oh, Galen, I'm sorry. I didn't mean to hurt your feelings. Please don't go."

"Why not? Because I might find someone else who'll help me and be nicer to me?"

"Galen, stop and think for a minute. This is an enchanted forest. You're not going to find anyone normal here. Anything you find will be dangerous. Pixie honor! Don't go!"

The clearing is very close now. You can see the small, plump figure of a little old woman seated before the fire. She has gray hair and plump rosy cheeks like your grandmother. A fat chicken is roasting on the fire.

"What kind of monster is that?" you demand.

"She's a witch, dummy," says Whimsy. "If you go to her, forget about the rest of your life. There won't be any. Don't expect me to help!"

"You're just jealous," you say angrily. But a small doubt creeps into your mind.

1) If you decide to enter the clearing, turn to page 33.

2) If you decide not to enter the clearing, turn to page 129.

"No! Why should I trust you?" you exclaim. "You're a dwarf! This is probably a trick to get me killed. Go away!"

The old dwarf tries hard to convince you that he is an enemy of the evil Sneed, but you are too scared and tired even to listen.

The old dwarf finally accepts the fact that he has lost. Sagging with defeat, he sinks to the floor and, wrapping his arms about his knees, mumbles softly to himself.

Early the next morning you are wakened by the sound of thousands of dwarves marching off to battle.

The old dwarf stands forlornly at the mouth of the empty cavern, listening to them go.

A thread of doubt creeps into your mind, and you wonder if maybe, just maybe, you made the wrong decision.

THE END

Although you would like to leap out and fight the dwarves, your parents have ordered you to stay hidden. You snuggle deep within the blankets and wrap your fingers tightly around Woofy's muzzle so that he cannot bark.

The wagon creaks as several dwarves climb into the cart near the front. You can hear them breaking open the boxes of supplies, looking for things of value.

Much as you wish to honor your parents' orders, you realize that the dwarves will find you soon. You must make another choice:

1) Fight the dwarves; turn to page 143.

2) Try to slip away; turn to page 59.

Somewhat afraid, you lie back down and try to go to sleep.

"Trust me," says Whimsy with a giggle.

"I won't be able to sleep a wink all night," you say. You hear a POOF! and that is the last you are able to remember of the night. You wake up in the morning to the smells of a wonderful breakfast.

"I bet that was the best night's sleep I ever had!" you say, stretching comfortably. Whimsy giggles but says nothing.

After you have eaten your fill, the three of you climb back up the winding tunnel, push back the trap door, and stand on the emerald moss of the forest floor, ready to continue your travels.

Please turn to page 94.

Ignoring Whimsy, you step into the clearing.

"Oh, how nice. Company for dinner," says the old woman. "Come right over here, you sweet little thing. I'll bet you're hungry and cold. Come warm yourself by my fire and help me eat this nice big chicken."

"Thank you. I'd like that very much."

"Here, dear, wrap yourself in this blanket. It will keep out the chill. And warm yourself with this nice cup of tea."

You see Whimsy's face fill with alarm. She gestures wildly from the edge of the forest.

In defiance, you lift the steaming cup to your lips and sip the fragrant brew. It warms you to the very tips of your tiny fingers and toes. You feel so warm and comfortable, you think it would be very nice to lie down on the soft blanket for just a minute.

You snuggle deep into its softness and close your eyes. The old lady pats you gently and says, "I'm so glad you dropped in, you tasty little morsel. I was wondering what to have for breakfast."

The pixie says sadly, "Oh, Woofy, why couldn't Galen have listened to me? I don't think I can do anything to help. The witch's powers are much stronger than mine."

Woofy whimpers softly and, with a last look at the cheery fire, the puppy and the pixie fade into the forest and disappear.

THE END

"Look, Woofy, here are the dwarves' tracks. Thanks to the rain, we won't have any difficulty following the trail. Maybe I can even teach you to be a tracking dog.

Woofy lays his ears flat against his head and growls. He seems to be looking at a heap of boulders that lies next to the trail.

"Come on, Woofy. Quit fooling around. This is serious! We've got to find those dwarves."

"You can stop looking, kid. You found us," growls a deep voice. And two of the largest, meanest-looking dwarves you've ever seen step out from behind the boulders.

"You grab the dog, Bulgar. I'll get the kid," says the larger of the two dwarves. Before you can even run, strong arms grab you and tie you up in a neat bundle.

"What do we need a dog for, Trog? It's not good for anything. Leave it here. Sneed never said anything about catching no dog. Besides, it might bite me," argues Bulgar.

Trog stands still, thinking and staring at Woofy, who growls and snarls at him.

"Yeah, you're right. Leave him here. But let's get this kid back to Sneed and collect our reward. If we hurry, we should get back to the caves by nightfall."

You struggle and kick, but the dwarves only laugh and throw you over their shoulders.

The dwarves walk steadily throughout the long day without stopping. As the sunset stains the ground red, Bulgar says, "Look, Trog, the caves. We're home."

"Good," grunts Trog. "This kid's heavy. A bowl of gopher stew will sure taste good."

The dwarves bend down, duck under a ledge, and enter a large cavern. Trog drops you to the ground, where you lie stunned.

Slowly your eyes become accustomed to the dim light. After a while you are able to make out the amazing features of the cavern.

The roof rises high above your head and twinkles like a miniature heaven filled with crystal stars. All along the walls, houses have been carved from solid rock. Each house is different. Some have walls made of glittering gems. Others have crystal windows above window boxes filled with mushrooms and fungus. All have lawns of smooth, soft moss.

Bearded dwarven women walk past, trying not to seem curious. But soon you are surrounded by a large crowd of dwarven children.

"It sure is ugly, isn't it?" says one.

"Yeah! Look at it! It doesn't even have a beard," says another in amazement.

"How can it stand to let anyone look at it," says a girl dwarf in a shocked voice. "I'd just hide in a cave and never come out if I didn't have a beard. It's so naked looking."

"Human children don't have beards."

A disbelieving gasp runs through the group.

"It talks," says a child who watches you with large, round eyes.

"Of course I talk. I may not have a beard, but I'm not stupid. Now why don't you let me loose so I can get out of here."

"Oh, we couldn't do that," whispers a small child, "not even if you had a beard." He looks over his shoulder fearfully, then turns back to you. "Sneed would be mad. Everyone is scared of Sneed, even the grown-ups. Some of our dads tried to argue with him once, but that was the last time they ever did it. Some of them got killed and the rest got locked up in the dungeons. So we can't help you."

"We would if we could," says another. "It would be nice to have a new friend."

"HEY! Get away from there!" yells a loud voice, and the children scatter like a flock of sparrows fleeing a falcon.

Long hours later, soft footsteps pad toward you. A sharp toe prods you in the back. Then a voice filled with menace says, "Thought you'd escape me, eh? Well, I always get what I want. Foolish child, you never had a chance."

"A thousand pardons, your worshipfulness," interrupts a whining voice, "but I have a progress report."

"Well, get on with it, Snively. Quit yapping about."

"Yes, sir. Yapping indeed. Very observant of you, sir."

"When do we march?" demands Sneed.

"Soon, sire, soon. I have labored without sleep for days now so that all will be in readiness. The smith is sharpening the last of the blades now. All will be done by morning."

"Soon all my enemies will be like dust before me, and I will be king," whispers Sneed.

"How glorious, sir! How magnificent! How splendid! Your greatness will outshine the sun itself and the city will be ours."

"Ours? Ours?" snarls Sneed.

"Yours! Yours alone! A tribute to your brilliance, oh wonderful one," whines Snively.

"Truly so, Snively. But we must be a little more modest. It is better understood by the masses. Take this child, for example. Does it appreciate watching the unfolding of history, the making of a king?"

"Speak up, brat! Answer when you're spoken to," hisses Snively.

"I see only a traitor!" you shout.

Snively draws a shocked breath and raises a hobnailed boot to kick you. But he's stopped by the sounds of a loud crash and angry voices echoing through the cave.

"It's that old fool, Hume Boulderbender! Why isn't he dead yet? What's he doing out of his cell, Snively?"

Peering into the gloom, you see an old, bent dwarf lying in a tumbled pile of spears. Several dwarves extend helping hands. But at a snarled warning from Sneed, they hurry away. The old dwarf regains his footing and, hands spread before him, begins to move unsteadily forward.

"It seemed pointless keeping him in his cell," cackles Snively. "As you can see, he is quite blind. Dwarves who might have remained loyal to their old king will see him as he is now and turn to us."

"Snively, I'm proud of you. Keep this up and one day, you might be worthy to follow in my footsteps," says Sneed. "But what of his son, Bork?"

"Still locked up in the deepest cells. One Boulderbender is more than enough!" Snively looks at you. "What shall I do with the brat? Drop it in a hole? Feed it to the wolves?"

"Do nothing," answers Sneed. "If we dispose of it, its father would probably refuse to map for me. Humans are so tiresome."

Poking you one last time, Sneed and Snively walk away.

All through the long evening and into the night you watch for something to happen that will allow you to escape. At last, you fall into an exhausted sleep on the cave floor.

You are awakened by a hand softly shaking your shoulder. "Wake up, child," whispers a deep voice. "Everything depends on you."

Startled, you open your eyes and see the old blind dwarf kneeling at your side.

A tattered robe covers the bent figure, and white hair flows into a massive beard. Bushy eyebrows hang over pale blue eyes that are covered with a thick, white film.

"Say that you will help," pleads the dwarf.

1) If you decide to trust the old dwarf, turn to page 47.

2) If you decide that you must not trust ANY dwarves, turn to page 30.

Marshy swamp replaces the grass banks, and clouds of insects whine in the weeds. The rest of the afternoon passes without event. Finally, Sandy says, "This looks like a good spot. Let's camp here tonight."

You enter a small cove and draw the raft up on the smooth, sandy beach. Thick forest presses in on all three sides. Dark tree trunks rise and are lost in a thick tangle of draping branches. Waxy white flowers hang in dense clusters and emit an overly sweet smell. Fat black leaves dangle downwards, twisting in the gentle breeze.

"I don't like this place," you say with a shiver. "It's creepy."

"I agree," says Sandy. "But this is the only clear spot we've seen in hours. We have to stay here for the night. I'm really tired and we have to find something to eat."

Reluctantly you agree and the two of you enter the dark forest. All about you are strange rustling noises and muted squeaks and growls.

The light grows dimmer with every step as you gather firewood and berries.

"Uh, Galen," Sandy finally whispers. "I think we have enough. Let's get back to the beach."

You are anxious to be out under the open sky. You feel unseen eyes on your back as you turn and hurry out of the forest.

"I think we should keep guard tonight," you say. "That forest is scary."

"I'll say!" says Sandy. "Look at Woofy."

Woofy lies with his head on his paws pointed straight at the forest. A ridge of fur stands on edge all along his spine. From time to time, he growls deep in his throat.

"Looks like we all agree," you say. "Well, I'll stand first watch. You get some sleep."

Sandy lies down by the fire and snuggles Woofy close to his chest.

"Don't worry, puppy," says Sandy. "We won't let anything get you." And soon both are asleep.

You try to stay alert and watchful, but it is difficult. The night is cloudy, and there is no moon. The river flows dark and quiet near your feet. Its waters look thick and black.

You give a shudder, glad that you are safe and warm on land. The shadowy forest itself is silent. Well, almost silent. You hear a curious breathing sound. In fact, it sounds as though the entire forest is breathing as one body. But that's impossible . . . isn't it?

Unfortunately, the sound is hypnotic and you drift off into a deep sleep.

You dream that you are floating through the sky on a soft, fluffy white cloud. The sky is a brilliant blue, and the air is sweet and fresh. It whispers by your ears with a gentle hiss. The hissing grows louder. It is so real that you can almost feel it as it brushes by your face. You reach up and your hand touches something firm. Something that moves. Something that is wrapping itself around your body!

You open your eyes and see a SNAKE! Its

thick, flat head is inches away from your face. Its large body is coiled loosely around your own. A terrified shock runs through you.

Jerking your gaze from the unblinking stare of the snake, you look towards Sandy and yell, "Sandy! Wake up! Snakes!"

All about you thick forms are dangling from the overhanging tree branches and slithering across the sand. You see by the glow of the campfire that several of the large reptiles are nearly upon Sandy and Woofy.

The snake begins to tighten its coils around your body. The breath is being forced from your lungs. Now the snake slithers over your head. Its muscles continue to squeeze. You cannot move your hands or feet. You can hear Sandy fighting the snakes. You can expect no help from him. You must help yourself if you are to live. Your breath is growing short. You are being squeezed to death.

1) You may try to roll into the river; turn to page 93.

2) You may try to roll into the embers of the fire; turn to page 91.

3) Or you may lie still and hope that Sandy rescues you; turn to page 10.

When the towers of the city finally appear, the horses are covered with foam and their breath is coming in huge, ragged sobs.

"Halt! Who goes there?" calls a sleepy voice from the town gate.

"Open in the name of the King's Guard," cries Bork boldly.

"What King's Guard?" questions the guard, peering over the edge of the gate tower. "I don't see any King's Guard. I see one young dwarf, one old dwarf, and one human kid. I don't like being waked in the middle of the night and I don't like jokes. And I don't care who you are. No one gets through this gate till I open it in the morning, and that's still an hour away. Now go away and let me get my sleep."

After shaking his fist one last time, he disappears from sight. No amount of pounding causes him to reappear.

You have two choices:

1) You can wait for the gate to open and risk the appearance of Sneed's army; turn to page 127.

2) Try to find another way into the city; turn to page 131

"I don't know how I can help. But I can't be any worse off than I am now," you say.

The old dwarf's fingers work with the rope and soon you are free. You rub your numb legs and then wobble to your feet.

"Here," says the dwarf, "I believe this is a friend of yours." Reaching into his worn robe, he pulls out a small, wiggly creature.

"Woofy, I was afraid I'd lost you forever!" you cry, flinging your arms around the puppy.

Calming the excited puppy, you say to the old dwarf, "We've got to stop Sneed!"

The old dwarf raises his hand and, soft as a whisper, touches your face. He seems to be memorizing your features by touch. Satisfied, the old dwarf takes your hands in his and looks at you with sightless eyes.

"Are you brave enough to trust me and go on a dangerous mission? If we succeed, we will stop Sneed, save the prince and your parents, and stop my people from doing a terrible wrong. But if we fail, it will mean our deaths.

"If you say no, I will understand and I will still help you rescue your parents. It is your choice."

1) If you decide to try to stop Sneed, turn to page 138.

2) If you decide just to rescue your parents and leave, turn to page 17.

You glare back at the ugly creature on whose back you stand. "Sandy, stand firm. I'm not going to let this big thing scare me. I'm sure we can bluff it."

"Oh, Galen, don't, please. Let's run for the raft. Come on, before it's too late. You don't bluff things this big."

"No, Sandy. My mind's made up. We've been terrorized by one thing after another on this river, and it's time to stop!

"Here, take Woofy and get to the raft. If you're so scared, I'll do it myself!"

You thrust the squirming puppy into Sandy's arms and stride bravely toward the head of the glaring monster.

"Now, see here," you holler. "We're not bothering you, and I'm not afraid of you. If you think I'm going to run away just because you're bigger than I am, you're wrong." And you whack the monster on its nose with your raft pole as hard as you can.

The monster roars with rage. The long neck snakes forward, and before you can run, the great beaked mouth closes about you.

Twisting as best you can, you raise your pole to your chest. You acted foolishly, but you're not dead yet, and with any luck, you'll escape to fight again another day.

THE END

"I have an idea," you say. "If we can get these two poles out of the raft, I'll bet we could use them just like spears."

Sandy looks at you with doubt. "Attack a dragon with wooden spears? Are you crazy?"

"No! Really! It would work. Trust me. All we have to do is be real quiet, position ourselves, and then—Blam! Dead dragon!"

"I don't think that's a good idea, Galen."

"Sandy, trust me. It'll work. I believed you when you said the raft would float. Now help me get these poles." Soon two poles are freed. You sharpen the ends with a pocket knife.

At that moment the raft wedges against one of the large rocks in the middle of the stream.

Gesturing for Sandy to follow, you step onto the spray-drenched stone.

"Follow me," you whisper as you clamber up the giant back. The scales twitch, but the dragon does not move. Slowly, the two of you inch your way along the rough, ridged spine.

At last you reach the junction of the great wings. "You stay here and find a place where you can work the point of your pole under a scale. I'm going up on its head. When I give the word, push as hard as you can. Trust me. It'll work."

Sun glints off the silvery black scales, which feel as hard as stone. You cling to the fearful beast's head.

Just as you are about to call to Sandy, one large eyelid opens slowly and an immense silver eye looks directly at you. The dragon stretches its enormous body. Clawed feet rise out of the muddy river and grip the rocks.

Lurching and swaying, the dragon rises to its feet. Your pole spins away. You grab the dragon's crest and hold on tightly. You are dangling between the dragon's eyes, both of which are now staring at you.

The dragon stretches once more and then yawns lazily. As he breathes out, bushes, small trees, and grass on the near bank fall and die.

Sandy struggles to keep his balance. Swaying wildly, he catches a silvery black shimmering wing and hangs on, clawing hand over hand, trying to save himself.

Never taking his eyes off you, the dragon twitches his wing and Sandy loses his grip and sails through the air. You see him strike the water and begin swimming for the shore.

Woofy barks wildly from the rocks below.

Suddenly the dragon sweeps Woofy up in one taloned claw. You watch in horror, unable to move, as ivory-white claws with razor-sharp edges reach toward you. You feel the claws curve around your body, and then you are plucked from the dragon's forehead.

The dragon settles its great bulk on the sun-warmed rocks and stares at you. You are surrounded by a warm cloud of bad-smelling gas. You hold your breath waiting for the flame or the bite that will end your life.

The dragon sighs again and says, "I don't understand you humans, always trying to kill

things. Even the largest, most dangerous dragon on the river. Haven't you ever heard the old saying, 'Let sleeping dragons lie'?"

You are numb with fear and cannot answer.

"Well, speak up, child. Can you talk?" asks the dragon, shaking you gently.

"No, sir. I mean, yes, sir. I mean, I'm sorry. Please don't eat me, sir," you squeak.

"Eat you? Of course I won't eat you. Humans upset my stomach. But I can't just let you go. It would ruin my reputation. If word got out, I'd be swamped by all sorts of stupid humans trying to kill me. And that would be a terrible nuisance.

"No, I'm afraid I'll just have to take you home to the caves and put you in with all the others I've collected over the years. The lodgings aren't the best, I suppose, but you'll be all right. One chap's been there, oh, long about fifty years now."

The dragon sighs deeply again and then, with you and Woofy clenched firmly in its scaly fist, shakes out its wings and prepares to launch itself into the skies.

"When will they ever learn?" the dragon mutters. "But then I must remember that humans are a lower form of life."

As the wind rushes by and the land falls far away beneath you, you wonder. . . Is this really

THE END?

"I don't think I want to get shrunk. If I go with you for a little while, can I come back?" you ask the dryad.

"Certainly, child," she says, swaying slightly in the wind.

"No! No! Don't do it. Don't believe her," cries Whimsy. "You can't trust dryads. You'll never come back. No fair, Liana. It's mine!"

Liana does not answer but laughs a sound like rustling leaves. She places a slender brown arm around you and draws you close, staring deeply into your eyes. You feel yourself falling, falling, falling.

Over the years—or are they centuries?—you experience wonders that few if any have ever seen before. You have become the heart of a great oak and waved your branches with wild joy in black, blinding storms. You have become a pebble at the bottom of a stream and watched the world wash by. You have been a cloud in the sky and listened to the heartbeat of the universe. But somehow it isn't enough. Occasionally you tell the tree spirit that you want to go home.

At last, Liana shrugs and leads you to a magic pool. "Look into this pool and you will see everything you want to know."

Leaning forward you peer anxiously into the pool. Reflected in the dark waters are the images of ruins. Ruins of cities with cold wind blowing through them. Ruins of dwarven areas empty of all life. Lands where monsters with strange shapes roam at will.

Finally, you rise from the pool. “I have seen enough. They have destroyed themselves through senseless warfare. It is no longer a place where I want to live. I cannot go back. I will stay with you forever if you will have me.”

Liana smiles at you, and you feel odd, somehow different.

Looking down you see that your hands are covered with bark. Your legs have become like tree trunks. You know in some distant corner of your mind that you should be worried, but somehow you're not. You laugh the laugh of rustling leaves. And taking Liana's hand in your own, you turn your back on the world of humans.

THE END

You continue on through the tunnel. Twice you jump when footsteps pound above your head. Finally you see light ahead. You crawl as fast as you can.

As you draw near the light, you see Woofy jumping up and down in a narrow, brick-lined area. Cries of "Sneed! Sneed! Sneed!" fill the air, and pike staffs thump on the cobblestones above you.

"What is all this?" cries a frightened voice. "Who are you and what do you want?"

"We want Sneed for king!" yell the dwarves.

Above you is a heavy metal grate. You find you can just touch it but not move it. Then several dwarves crowd onto the grate.

"Hey! You up there. Help me!" you cry, but your shouts go unheard.

Then you hear voices off to one side. "No, prince, don't go. They're rabble!"

"Hush, Mabbit. They're part of my kingdom. If there is a problem, I should know about it."

The small, clear voice rings out, "You have a problem? Well, I'm here. Let's talk!"

The feet above your head shuffle nervously. Then a gruff voice cries, "We don't want no kid for king. We want Sneed!"

You call again, "Help! Help! Look down! Get me out of here!" but nobody listens.

Then you hear another dwarf shout, "You stole our land. We want Sneed! You humans don't care about dwarves."

"I never stole anything from anyone. Maybe

I don't understand dwarves, but I'll learn."

"You did so steal our land. We're slaves in our own mountain. What used to be ours now belongs to you. Thief! Thief! Thief!"

"Let's get him," shouts a voice, and the crowd surges forward.

You are nearly frantic with fear for the prince. You know the true story of the mountain, but it will not do the prince any good if you cannot escape from the storm drain.

Suddenly, something thumps you on the back of the neck. It's a small stone. It didn't fall from above. You would have seen it. You examine your surroundings closely. On the wall at head height is a small pipe. Out of it comes the prince's voice. "Stop! Don't throw rocks at me. We can settle our differences if we talk. Ouch!"

His voice is very clear. It sounds as though he is standing in front of you talking to you.

You have an idea! Putting your mouth against the pipe you say in a loud, deep voice, "STOP THROWING ROCKS! PUT DOWN THOSE STONES! Shame on you."

You are very pleased to hear your voice, magnified by the pipe, rolling over the crowd.

Suddenly all is silent. You have a choice:

1) If you wish to keep tricking the dwarves, turn to page 123.

2) If you wish to tell somebody to rescue you, turn to page 104.

"I think I'd rather stay here. I don't like the other two choices," you say.

"And I don't like cowards," roars Orff in anger. "There's no place for you in my kingdom." And pointing his finger at you, there is a POOF! and suddenly you find yourself standing in a strange, underground cave surrounded by thousands of angry pixies and a growling dog. They are all very angry at you, but you don't know why. In fact, you don't even remember who you are or what you are doing here.

Shaking your head in confusion, you head up a tunnel and find yourself in a strange forest. As you walk into the wilderness, you wonder if you will ever remember who you are and why you are wandering in this giant forest.

THE END

You grasp Woofy firmly and wriggle toward the end of the cart. You peek over the edge and see that the guards are all facing away from you. With luck, you will be able to escape without being seen into the rocky hillside that borders the trail.

You slip over the edge of the cart and are nearly into the safety of the rocks when Woofy begins to bark in excitement.

"Look over there! It's a kid. Catch it! Don't let it get away!" screams Sneed, the guard captain.

"Run, Galen! Run-n-n-n-n!" cries your father, fear for you in his voice.

"You stupid dog. Dwarves can see in the dark. They'll be able to spot us even at night," you say angrily to Woofy as you begin to run.

Your words are drowned out by a tremendous noise crashing all around you. A brilliant sheet of lightning rips the night sky, and rain begins to fall heavily.

Fighting the rain, the steep hillside, and the weight of the wiggling puppy, you climb as fast as you can. But huge boulders litter the hillside, and the going is difficult.

The rain becomes a downpour, and the ground is very slippery. All at once your feet slip out from under you and you crash to the ground. Fortunately, you don't land on any rocks, but Woofy slips eagerly from your grasp and disappears into the darkness.

"Blasted dog! I should have left him behind," you mutter. "He thinks it's all a game.

Still, if I don't find him, he'll start barking and lead them right to me. Woofy! Woofy, where are you?" you whisper loudly.

You can hear the dwarves calling to each other. They are moving nearer and nearer. Soon they will be upon you.

"Woofy!" you whisper urgently, crawling about on hands and knees.

A warm wetness wipes itself across your face. A wriggling, wet, furry body crashes into you. "Woofy, come here, boy." But the puppy disappears. Then, sharp teeth nip your ankle and tug at your boot.

"Woof," says an oddly muffled puppy voice. Peering into the darkness beneath the overhang of an enormous boulder, you see two white eyes. "Woof, woof!" yips Woofy happily.

"This isn't a game, you silly puppy, but you may have saved our lives."

Lying flat on the muddy ground, you scrape and claw your way under the overhang. You are almost too big, but dwarf voices and heavy footsteps urge you to squeeze your way in.

Seconds later stumpy dwarf feet pause mere inches from your face.

"Which way did the brat go, Snively?"

"I don't know, sir. I tried to see, but I lost sight when the lightning struck, sir. I'm sure I'll find the trail in a minute, sir. I'm not as strong as you are, but I'm a good tracker, sir," says a whining voice.

"Bah! Snively, you're disgusting. Quit whining. Get out of here and find that kid."

"Yes, Captain, sir. I probably am disgusting, sir, but I try hard, sir."

There is the sound of steel being drawn.

"Oh, no, sir. No need for swords, sir. I'll go. Don't you worry, sir. If there's a track, I'll find it, sir."

"Then get out of here and go find it," yells Sneed.

"Yes, sir," yelps Snively, scrambling away.

Sneed's feet move off, leaving only two dwarves near your hiding place.

You hear one of them complain, "I don't understand why Sneed lets that worm Snively hang around. I can't stand him. One day I'll spit him on my sword."

"Don't bother," says the other dwarf. "He's not worth the effort. Come on. We'd better find that kid or it'll be us spitted on Sneed's sword. We can't afford for anyone to escape and carry a warning to the prince."

The hours crawl slowly by as angry dwarves explore the rocky hillside looking for you. A dozen times muddy feet stop near your face. You fear discovery. But luck is on your side and not a single dwarf face peers into yours.

Just as you begin to doubt that they will ever give up, a pair of leather boots stop before your hiding place.

"How can you have failed?" shrieks a familiar frightening voice. "I will not accept failure. Someone will pay for this!"

"Captain, we've searched everywhere," pleads a tired voice. "It's wild country out there. The kid's probably dead by now or soon will be."

"Pray you're right. If that kid lives to carry a warning to the prince, all will be over for us. Our only future will be disgrace and death. Snively! Where are you?"

"Here, sir. Always at your side, sir."

"What say you, Master Tracker, Master Fool? Can't you even find one small child?"

"Yes, sir. If you please, sir. I tried, sir, but the rain, sir. And the men walked all over what tracks there were."

"Faugh!" Sneed spits angrily. "You couldn't find your nose in a mirror."

"Oh, yes, sir. I know, sir," moans Snively.

"Enough of this. Back to the horses. There's much to be done. Post armed guards along the road. I want that child found!"

"Not a minute too soon," grumbles a dwarf. "I'm soaked to the bone."

Slowly the complaining voices fade away.

Outside, the rain gusts and the wind wails. But you are warm, dry, and safe—for the moment. Slowly, your heavy lids close. You curl up beside Woofy and are soon fast asleep.

Hours later, you are dreaming of eating a great feast when you waken to Woofy licking your face and tugging at your hair.

Protecting yourself from the puppy's greeting, you sit up and stretch. Your head bumps solid stone, and memory of the horrible night just past floods back upon you.

"Well, Woof. I guess it wasn't a dream," you

say, rubbing your head. "I guess I'd better do something. But what?

1) "Maybe I should follow the dwarves and try to rescue my folks." Turn to page 34.

2) "Or maybe I should head across country to find grown-ups and try to get them to help." Turn to page 86.

3) "Or maybe I can reach the city and warn the prince." Turn to page 19.

The creature is squeezing you very, very hard, but you manage to reach your knife. You begin to stab and hack at its hand.

The golem stops for a minute and then shakes you so hard that the knife falls from your hand. Then the monster raises you high and, drawing his arm back, throws you from him in one powerful motion. Tops of trees rush by you as you fly through the air. Then you see an immense tree rising up ahead of you. With a crash of broken branches you come to rest in the top of the trees. Thankfully, although you are bruised and shaken, you have no broken bones.

Parting the leaves, you look down. Your heart seems to stop as you realize how high up you are. Somewhere in this forest are Woofy and Whimsy and the golem. Somehow, you must get down to the ground and find them . . . if it's not too late.

THE END

"I hope this works," mutters Sandy as he takes off his vest and hangs it on the torch.

"I hope so, too!" you cry, dodging the rush of a bold rat. Woofy barks from the safety of your arms.

"Look, Galen! Look at them go!" yells Sandy as he thrusts his flaming vest at the rats.

"Hooray!" you yell as the swamp rats jibber and twitter, crawling over each other in fear.

In just seconds the last naked pink tail has disappeared over the edge of the raft.

The vest gives one last burst of flame and then is gone You are in the dark once more.

Woofy gives a strangled bark, and you realize that you are squeezing him tightly. Putting the puppy down, you say shakily, "By the gods, Sandy, I'm glad you thought of that. Truly, I thought we were dead. They're such ugly creatures! We were lucky to escape them."

"I wonder what more this river has in store for us," whispers Sandy. "I longed for adventure, but now, my old straw bed would look good. I'd even be glad to see Grundge."

"Come on, don't be so sad. We're OK. We're alive. What else could possibly happen to us before we can get to the city? And then we'll warn the prince and rescue my folks, and everything will be wonderful."

"I guess you're right," says Sandy. "But I'm hungry and I'm scared."

You sigh deeply. In your heart you feel the same way. "Sandy, I don't know what else to say. I need you. I couldn't do this without you.

If I were by myself, I'd be so scared I'd give up. Don't quit now. Everything will be better in the morning. Trust me."

"Do you really think so?" asks Sandy.

"I don't know, but I hope so. I mean, what else could happen to us? Snakes! Rats! Dragons! Let's go to sleep. We'll just have to believe that we're going to be OK."

You settle yourself as comfortably as possible, tuck Woofy's head down on your shoulder, and say to Sandy, "Try not to worry any more. Go to sleep. Tomorrow's another day."

Woofy whines and looks at the dark water.

"Stop it, Woof. Nothing's going to get us."

For a time you stare out at the dark night, wondering what it holds. Finally sleep claims you, and you rest deeply without dreams.

As the tiny craft floats on the rushing water, heavy-lidded eyes atop scaly snouts watch your progress before submerging once again.

Throughout the long night, the raft drifts silently down the river. You are watched by many, but no one stops you. As pink streaks begin to work their way across the night sky, the raft moves between ever-narrowing banks. Trees and rushes give way to rocks and boulders. The waters rush more swiftly and currents clash violently.

Sandy yawns, sits up, and rubs his eyes. "Galen, wake up. We're alive and I have this feeling that everything's going to be all right!"

You sit up slowly. Your body aches all over. You are sure you haven't slept more than a few minutes. Groaning, you start to turn over when suddenly your eyes pop open. The calmly drifting raft is now rushing along at a dizzying speed, being pulled by powerful currents.

High stone cliffs rise on either side of the river, and a dull roar can be heard. It seems to be in front of you. You don't know what it means, but it doesn't sound good. The water rushes faster.

"All right? I wouldn't count on anything being all right just yet, Sandy. Let's try to steady the raft, maybe pole over to the side. That way if we don't like what's coming up, we'll have a chance to get off."

Without a word, Sandy picks up his pole. Both of you plunge your poles into the swirling water. "Galen, I can't reach bottom. It's too deep. What do we do?"

"Try to use your pole like a paddle," you yell. "We'll try to move the raft that way."

Quickly dropping to the floor of the wildly pitching raft, the two of you try desperately to paddle toward the side. Fear of the increasing roar adds strength to your strokes. But the walls slip by faster and faster as the raft races with the wild river. Woofy howls in fear as the raft tilts crookedly.

The roaring grows ever louder, and a thick mist begins to cloud the air.

"Sandy, I don't know what it is, but I think we're in trouble."

"I think it's a waterfall. That's what it sounds like."

Before you can answer, a dark shape looms up out of the mist. As the river carries you swiftly forward, you see a small island rising out of the water. The rock parts the water like a ship moving upstream, the water splitting into swift, narrow channels.

"Oh, my gosh!" gasps Sandy. "It IS a waterfall. What shall we do, Galen?"

You cross to his side, and the two of you stare as disaster comes nearer and nearer.

"Look, Sandy. Over there on the left the water drops straight down. And on the right there's a whole bunch of boulders.

"We've only got three choices, none of them good.

1) "We can go to the left, go straight over the waterfall, and hope for the best." If this is your choice, turn to page 147.

2) "We can go to the right and hope the boulders ease the force of the water." If this is your choice, turn to page 84.

3) "We can aim for the island and get off there. That way we don't have to go down the waterfall at all." If this is your choice, turn to page 18.

The magic symbols must mean something, maybe even something very important, to the golem. Maybe if you messed up the words you could mess up the monster.

A slash of lightning tears across the sky outlining the fearsome creature. Reaching over, you slash your knife through the carving.

In the blink of an eye, the golem's arms freeze. You are left hanging in midair. Somehow you manage to wriggle out of the wooden fist.

A shout of joy tells you that Whimsy has also succeeded in freeing herself. You crawl down the gnarled, muscular, wooden arm and then down the bark-covered body to the ground. Woofy leaps happily at your feet.

"That was wonderful! You're almost as clever as I am," says Whimsy, jumping up and down with glee. "How did you know to do that? I didn't know you knew any magic."

Your chest fills with pride, but reluctantly you admit, "I don't know any magic. I just figured that those symbols wouldn't have been there if they weren't important."

"I'm so glad it worked and we didn't get smashed. But my ribs will be sore for a week," moans Whimsy. "Let's get out of here before something comes to see what happened."

The thought of another monster is so awful the three of you turn and run into the forest.

Please turn to page 109.

"Look, Sandy. I know you wanted adventure, but this is too much for me. I think we'd better give this up and turn around and go back. How can I help my folks and the prince if I'm in a dragon's stomach?"

"I guess you're right," says Sandy slowly, "but I still think we could have done it."

Quietly you and Sandy slip into the water and swim for the right shore. You watch as the raft drifts between two large rocks, catches for a moment, then breaks free to whirl away downstream. The dragon slumbers on.

The two of you walk silently back to the clearing where you met. Woofy frolics at your feet, but neither of you feels like playing.

"I guess it's good-bye," says Sandy, holding out his hand. "Good luck with the dwarves."

You shake his hand and mumble, "Thanks for everything. Sorry we lost your raft."

"That's all right," says Sandy. "I can make another one. It wasn't so hot anyhow."

You walk off down the path, retracing the steps you took earlier. As you and Woofy wind your way through the meadow, Sandy's voice follows you. "I still think we should have tried it. I think we would have made it!"

You don't turn and you don't answer. Your stomach feels bad, and you wonder if maybe Sandy was right. But you will never know.

Please turn to page 34.

There seem to be hundreds of little furry bodies struggling to reach you. You take a deep breath, clasp Woofy firmly, and leap into the river. Before you even strike the water, you sense Sandy beside you. The water is warm, so swimming isn't too hard.

As you slosh through the rushes that line the shore, you turn and catch a last glimpse of the rat-covered raft floating down the river.

"What are we going to do now?" asks Sandy as you collapse wearily on the weedy bank.

"I don't know," you sigh, "but at least we got rid of those rats. They scared me even worse than the snakes. I just had to get away from them."

At that moment, Woofy begins to growl and crawls into the security of your lap. Briefly the clouds move away from the moon and a beam of light illuminates red eyes and white teeth and little furry bodies—thousands of them! And then you hear it . . . the mindless chittering and nattering of the swamp rats.

You may have escaped those few on the raft, but now you are surrounded. Is this . . .

THE END?

You bend low over the horse's neck and urge it forward. But the animal is unfamiliar with you and, to your horror, begins to slow down! You jab your heels in the horse's ribs and he jumps forward, and then bucks violently. A quick look back tells you that the guard is gaining fast. He will be on you within seconds!

Miraculously, Bork appears at your side and rides back to meet the guard. Bork gives him no opportunity to use either sword or dagger. With a powerful blow, he sweeps the dwarf off his horse and into the flood of stampeding animals. The riderless horse rushes away and is gone.

Without waiting to see the fate of the fallen dwarf, the three of you turn and race away toward the distant city. Dawn is near and the dwarven army will soon be on the march.

Please turn to page 45.

No sooner have you agreed than six pixies swoop down, grasp you firmly, and zoom off.

You watch in fear and awe as the roof of the forest slips beneath you. Suddenly, without warning, the pixies swoop, twirl, and dive steeply! The tops of the trees rise to meet you. You will surely die!

Just as you are able to see individual leaves clearly, the pixies pull up sharply and soon you are safe above the trees once more.

"Why did you do that?" you yell. "You scared me half to death! No more tricks! Just get me to the castle as soon as possible!"

Although they snicker and giggle a lot, the pixies play no more tricks. Soon the towers of the city rise out of the morning mist. The city gates are closed and patrolled by armed guards.

The palace looms up out of the mist. There's a guard at every gate. The pixies fly over the barred gates and head for an open window in the very tallest tower. You find yourself in a large, round room. In the center is a big bed with someone sleeping in it.

The pixies hover for a moment, drop you on the bed, and then sit giggling at its foot.

The figure sits up, yawns, and rubs its eyes. You realize with a shock that it's the prince!

Sleepy eyes open wide in disbelief. "Are you real, or am I dreaming?"

The pixies laugh aloud and begin to bounce up and down on the bed.

"I guess I'm not dreaming," says the prince, as the bed bounces beneath him.

"Stop that," you command sharply, and the pixies scramble off the bed and begin exploring the room. "No, sire, you're not dreaming. We're very real. I'm Galen and these are my friends the pixies. They've brought me here so that I could warn you about the dwarves. They're massing in the hills readying for war. They plan to capture the kingdom and kill you."

The prince cries out, "What can we do?"

"The pixies have a plan," you answer. "If you alert the army, the pixies will help. They can shoot tiny arrows that cause instant forgetfulness. If your soldiers attack in front and the pixies from above, we could win."

"But won't the dwarves see the pixies and shoot them down before they can get close?"

"Watch," you say with a smile. "Pixies, show the prince why you won't be seen." Pixies come scurrying out of the many corners of the room and line up in a row. "One, two, three," you count, and then POOF! they all disappear.

"Where are they? Where did they go?" The prince kneels on his bed and looks under the quilt.

A fit of giggling bursts from the spot where the pixies disappeared.

The prince leaps out of bed and, bending over, gingerly touches the invisible pixies.

"They're here! But they're invisible!"

"That's why our plan will work," you say.

"I'll go rouse the army. There's no time to

lose," cries the prince as he runs out the door.

"Prince! Come back! You're still in your pajamas," you call, but the prince is gone.

Sighing, you turn to the invisible pixies. "Well, at least he's convinced. Now we'd better get back and tell King Orff what's happened."

You feel yourself lifted by twelve little invisible hands. The pixies fly out the window, circle the tower, zoom over the heads of the guards, and zip through the center of town. The city gates are just being opened as you approach at breakneck speed. As you pass between the gates, you look down at the two guards who are pushing open the heavy doors and politely say, "Good morning," tipping your hat as you fly by.

One stares at you—a pixie-sized human seemingly hanging in midair—speechless. But the second pulls his hat over his eyes and cries, "Witchcraft!" and runs away as fast as he can.

Soon you stand before Whimsy, Woofy, and King Orff. "We did it!" you exclaim happily.

"Good!" cries the king. "And we're ready here. So let's be on our way."

Whimsy steps forward and places a large orange trumpet flower to her lips. A melody both urgent and sweet pours from the trumpet flower.

Suddenly the woods are filled with the rustling and giggling of thousands of pixies. They peer at you from between leaves, behind

trees, and beneath bushes. Big pixies, little pixies, thin pixies, and fat pixies. Pixies dressed in all shades of the rainbow. And all of them armed with little bows and quivers filled with tiny, sharp arrows.

When at last King Orff is satisfied that all the pixies have arrived, the tiny winged army begins to move. Brightly colored pixies flit through the air like jeweled hummingbirds and glistening dragonflies. You ride astride Woofy at the head of the advancing army. Soon you and the pixies are gathered at the edge of the forest before an open plain.

"We will stay here until it is time," says Orff, and your army settles down to wait.

All too soon, you sense a low rumbling noise. It's the beat of dwarven drums. The dread sound echoes through the forest and pours over the plain. All around you pixies tend to last minute duties, checking weapons and wings.

Sooner than you might have wished, the dwarves march onto the plain. Bearded, brawny, and armor-clad, they march in a solid mass. The excited pixies are held back by a sign from their king.

A horn blares as the city gates open wide and the prince's army pours out.

"NOW!" yells Orff, and the air is filled with thousands of POOFS. All of the brightly colored pixies disappear in a flash, and the air is filled with the beating of tiny wings.

A few dwarves look up, sensing something,

but they see nothing. And then, the pixies begin to shoot their arrows. Many strike armor and fall to the ground. But soon the effect of those that strike flesh can be easily seen. Horses, screaming with panic, begin crashing into one another, disrupting the dwarven advance.

Soon the plain is filled with dazed dwarves who cannot remember who they are or what they are supposed to be doing.

The prince's army gallops onto the plain and joins the battle. Throughout the long fight, the pixies continue shooting at dwarves and occasionally at humans, just for fun.

As night falls, the battle ends. The prince calls you to him.

"Galen, we are victorious this day only because of your bravery and that of the pixies. You have my everlasting thanks. Even the dwarves will not suffer unjustly. There must be some reason behind this revolt. I will try to find out what it is, and if it is fair, I will right the wrong. Also, I have sent a company of my best men to free your parents. They should be with us soon. I know they will be proud of you."

A warm, happy feeling spreads through you. You have tried something really difficult and succeeded. You will be sad to leave the pixies, but you are glad to know that everything will be fine once more.

THE END

You cling desperately to the raft as it plummets over the edge and plunges through the foaming waters. Water hammers your body as you and the raft fall into nothingness. Your eyes are blinded by the water and you can scarcely breathe. Then, with a bone-jarring impact, the raft crashes into a pool of water, and, to your horror, begins to break apart.

Sandy struggles to your side and gasps, "Grab a log, Galen, and hang on tight!" just as a huge surge of water washes him away.

You lock your arms tightly around a large log. No sooner have you taken a deep breath than the current seizes you again and pushes you over the next step. Try as you might, you cannot hold on to the log, and soon it is torn from your grasp.

Afraid of drowning, afraid of being hit by the logs from the raft, and afraid of crashing into river rocks, you bounce from one level to the next.

At last, battered and exhausted, you are washed into a quiet pool at the foot of the waterfall.

Please turn to page 12.

Cautiously you edge into the left-hand tunnel. The sound of rushing water grows louder. You are trying to move with care when suddenly your hands slip on a patch of slick moss. You feel yourself beginning to slide. All at once the pipe ends and you drop through cold, dark space. Splash! You plunge deep into swiftly flowing icy water that seizes you in its powerful current and whirls you away.

You have fallen into the great underground river that flows beneath the city.

You are pushed along by the fierce current and deposited, bruised and battered, on the banks of the river as it surfaces miles beyond the walls of the city.

You crawl up onto a muddy bank. You lie there panting and trying to think. You could walk back to the city and maybe still help. You could also try to walk back to the caves and free your parents while most of the dwarves are gone. But either way, you realize, you are probably too late to save the prince.

THE END

Carefully you look out from beneath the rock overhang, but you see no one.

"Woofy? Where are you? Come on. Let's go." Then as the puppy appears from under the rock, you add, "Really, Woof, you've got to learn to come when I call you. You're in there playing games and I'm ready to go. Be more serious!"

Woof puts his head to one side and looks at you strangely. For just a brief moment you think you hear laughter, but you listen carefully and the tiny sound is not repeated.

"Must be the wind," you say, and you set off across the rocky hillside.

The two of you climb for several hours, and slowly the harsh, gray land gives way to gently rolling hills covered with soft grass and bright flowers.

Soon you find yourself in a pleasant valley where woolly white sheep dot the hillsides.

"Look. Over there, Woof. It's smoke! Come on, we're bound to find someone who'll help us." And you race eagerly toward the small stone house at the end of the pretty valley.

As you approach the small building, you begin to notice its shabby appearance. Rags are stuffed into broken windows. The door hangs loosely on its hinges, and the yard is filled with trash. Sitting on the doorstep is a large man dressed in torn, unwashed clothing.

Seeing you, he grabs a large wooden club.

"What do you want here?" he roars, shaking his club at you.

"Please, sir," you stammer. "I need help. I mean . . . my parents need help . . . and the prince needs help. You see, the dwarves . . . " And the tale tumbles out of you.

"What do I care about princes and dwarves and helping other folks. Get off my land!"

"But you've got to help!" you cry in despair. The club is raised menacingly and the big man takes another step toward you.

Woofy rushes off, tail between his legs, toward the forest that stands near the house.

"Please, sir," you plead hopefully.

"Off!" roars the man and throws his club straight at you. You duck quickly as it whizzes overhead. Curses and threats follow your flight into the forest. Only when you can no longer hear the man's voice do you slow down. You stumble into a small clearing and find Woofy waiting for you. Collapsing on a large, flat rock, you clutch the puppy to you and bury your face in his warm fur.

"Oh, Woof, what am I going to do now?"

"Maybe I can help," says a strange voice.

Instantly you leap to your feet, dropping the puppy. "Yip Yip!" complains Woofy.

"Are you all right, little fella?" asks the stranger, who picks up the puppy. "He's cute. What's his name?"

"Woofy. What's yours?"

"I'm Sanders Goodfellow, though most folks call me Sandy. I guess you can see why."

A boy about your own age and size stands before you. Unevenly cut sand-colored hair

frames a square face that is almost completely covered with freckles. Brown eyes outlined with thick blond lashes and brows gaze directly into your own. A blunt pug nose tops a wide, smiling mouth. The sleeves of a sturdy brown homespun shirt fail to cover the wrists of the lanky figure. Large bony fingers hold Woofy, who is doing his best to wash the stranger's face.

"I heard you talking to Squire Grundge and I thought I'd see if maybe I could help. He won't help anyone—he's too mean. There's hardly anything for me to do except tend the sheep. And they don't really need me at all. Would you let me come along? I could be a big help."

You study the boy suspiciously for a moment, but he seems so honest you decide to trust him.

"I don't want to mess with those dwarves," says Sandy. "But if you want to try to warn the prince, I think I can get you there by river. I've got a boat of my own. I've never been to the city, but I think the river goes that far."

1) If you would like to try to reach the city and the prince by way of the river, turn to page 134.

2) If you decide that the river route sounds too chancy, pick up Woofy and bid Sandy farewell. Return to the boulder and try to follow the dwarves. Turn to page 34.

"I'm afraid of Sneed, too, sir, but I will help you free your son," you say to the old dwarf.

You follow him through many tunnels, traveling deeper and deeper into the mountain.

"How do you know where we're going? Are we lost?" you ask fearfully.

"I've spent my life within this mountain. Even without sight, I know every inch of it as well as you know your own home. Do not fear."

You walk on through damp and musty tunnels dimly lit by glowing rock. Finally, Hume clutches your arm gently and whispers, "We're nearing the lowest level. It is here that Bork is kept under constant guard."

"How do we rescue him if he's guarded?" you ask.

"I don't know. We'll just have to think of something," says Hume.

You reach the end of the corridor and, peering around the corner, you see a sturdy door that is barred and padlocked. Before the door stands a muscular dwarf holding a large club. A sword and a dagger hang from his belt.

1) If you want to try to attack the dwarf, turn to page 121.

2) If you want to try to trick the dwarf, turn to page 9.

Gasping at the musky smell of the snake, you feel the thick coils of the giant reptile wrap around your entire body.

Fear and pain engulf you, but you know that if you do not do something, you will soon be dead. Fighting panic, you try to remember where the fire is. You use the last of your breath and strength to roll yourself and the snake straight into the glowing embers of the campfire.

Writhing in pain, the snake hisses loudly. The scent of scorched snake flesh is strong. The air feels hot, but the snake's great bulk protects you from the heat of the fire.

The snake's great coils slowly loosen from your chest. You wriggle free and push yourself away from the snake and the fire.

Staggering to your feet, you see a giant snake, its skin mottled with burned patches, slithering into the forest.

Please turn to page 113.

The pixie flies in front of you, hovering like a gem in the clear morning air. Although you are much larger than she is and have very long legs, you find it hard to keep up with her. Woofy has no such problems and frolics easily alongside. Finally, the tiny creature settles astride Woofy's neck and directs him with gentle knee pressure.

You are almost at the foot of the hill when Whimsy stops Woofy abruptly and hisses, "Get down."

You look around in all directions and see nothing but rocks and your burned wagon. "Why? There's nothing around here that can hurt us."

"Get down, you silly human! There are two dwarves hiding behind that big boulder next to the trail."

Dropping to the ground, you stare intently at the rocks but see no sign of dwarves.

"What should we do?" you ask.

"Leave it to me. I'll fix them," says Whimsy as she strings a tiny bow.

1) If you want to leave the matter in the pixie's hands, turn to page 116.

2) If you want to ignore the pixie's advice and attack the dwarves, turn to page 146.

Exerting every muscle in your body, you roll yourself over and over until you and the snake splash into the water. The current seizes you and you are rushed away into the darkness.

Almost immediately you smash to a stop. Your feet touch a hard, rough bottom. You realize that you have crashed into rocks. Using your last breath, you struggle to your feet and bash yourself and the snake against them. The snake tightens its coils about you, but you continue to batter it against the rocks.

You are dizzy, and red and green flashes burst against the inside of your eyelids. You cannot fight any longer, but at least you did the best you could.

You are sinking into fuzzy blackness, a quiet, safe place, when you realize that the bands of steel are relaxing. Scarcely daring to hope, you try to move your hands and find that you can! With what little strength you have left, you free your hands and pull the snake away from your face. You gulp in the air in great, deep breaths.

The great snake stirs sluggishly and tries to tighten itself about you again, but before it can do so, you seize its head and bash it against the rocks. The giant reptile rips itself away and swims off into the night.

Weary and aching from head to toe, you swim back to the camp, wondering what you will find.

Please turn to page 113.

You step on a rock and climb up behind Whimsy on Woofy's back. After a short time, the sky clouds over and rain begins to fall.

Lightning rips through the sky and thunder booms about you. Abruptly the forest thins and you enter a clearing. You are looking for shelter when you notice a strange double-trunked tree in the center of the clearing. It stands eight feet high, and its branches are bare of leaves. It looks almost dead.

"Let's head for that tree," shouts Whimsy. "There's probably a dry spot between its roots."

You don't like the looks of the tree, but there doesn't seem to be a better choice.

You reach the strange tree and huddle between the two trunks. Suddenly you realize that you and Whimsy are wedged tightly against each other.

"Whimsy, am I imagining it or is this space getting smaller?" you ask nervously.

As you speak, the two rain-soaked trunks begin squeezing together. Only with great difficulty are you able to pull yourselves free.

As you stumble forward, something grabs you around the waist and lifts you high into the air. A scream from Whimsy tells you that she, too, has been caught. You see a large, ugly face staring at you through the rain. A heavy, thick forehead with eyebrows stuck full of twigs hangs over crazed eyes. A crooked nose curves over the thin gash of a mouth.

The monster glares at you and squeezes you

even more tightly. You pound on the barked hand. It has no effect. As you struggle in the giant fist, you realize that the creature has been created from a living tree. Strange symbols are carved above its face.

"Whimsy! What is this thing? How can we get loose?" you scream. "I can't breathe!"

"It's a wood golem. My spells won't work on it. Nor will my weapons. Those marks on its forehead are magic symbols. We've got to try to stop it somehow. And I've only got one idea."

The golem raises you higher. You are afraid that it is going to throw you to the ground.

You have three choices:

1) Tell Whimsy to try her only idea; turn to page 124.

2) Try to scratch the symbols off the monster's forehead and hope that it will somehow kill the monster's magic; turn to page 71.

3) Take your knife and hack at the wooden hand imprisoning you; turn to page 65.

"I'm sorry, but I can't leave my parents. I have to free them. You go on without me."

Bork tells you how to find the prison and with a sinking heart, you watch the two dwarves walk away down a dark corridor.

Following Bork's instructions, you are able to find your parents' cell. With difficulty you remove the heavy bar and are soon at their side.

"Oh, Galen!" cries your mother. "I thought we would never see you again."

"Where have you been? How did you escape?" asks your father.

Quickly you tell them all you have learned of the dwarves and their plot.

"Galen, you must leave us and go back to Bork and Hume. Sneed will succeed if they do not stop him. You must help them if you can," says your father. Then he adds thoughtfully, "Do you remember the old drainage system? That might be a way into the city. Once you warn the prince, you can come back for us. If we leave, Sneed will know the game is up and move more quickly."

"No!" sobs your mother. "It's too dangerous. You could be killed! Don't go!"

1) If you want to help the dwarves, hug your mother and turn to page 106.

2) If you want to stay with your parents, turn to page 108.

"But how will we get past the guards?"

"No one stop lizardmen," hisses the reptile.

The air around you is filled with hisses, grunts, and bellows. Scaly forms slither out of the water, answering the call of their brothers. "Climb on back. We go!"

Each of you straddles a bumpy back and soon you are wending your way through the gloomy swamp. As brown waters sweep by, you see that you would never have escaped.

Soon the spires of the city can be seen as the swamp gives way to tall brown grasses.

The grass hides you, and you are able to come very near the entrance to the city.

"Look! Guards everywhere. We'll never get in," cries Sandy in despair.

"Guards not stop lizardmen," hisses Squamata. Suddenly the air is filled with bellows, hisses, and grunts. The guards clutch their spears and look about in fear. Still making the fearful noises, the reptiles advance upon the terrified guards who run through the gates and start to close them.

The lizardmen move steadily forward. Squamata slams one huge armored fist forward, and the massive gates crash open.

"Head for the palace!" you yell.

Patrols of astonished guards are met and tossed aside. A few spears are thrown, but they bounce off the bony hides of the lizards.

"One hundred gold coins to the dwarves who stop those creatures!" shouts a dwarven chief. But the marching lizardmen cast the little dwarves aside like falling leaves.

Entering the palace, Squamata seizes a fleeing noble. "Get prince! He talk to us now." He gives the terrified noble a final shake and puts him down with a thump.

"It's all right. Please do as he says," you yell after the racing figure.

Rows of reptiles fill the throne room, seething restlessly. Suddenly, there is a quick movement near the throne. A small boy holding a sword much too big for him and a shield he can barely lift walks to the edge of the platform. Behind him stands Sneed.

"Well, well, my good lizardmen," smiles Sneed. "This is an unexpected pleasure. Why are we so honored?"

"Villain! Traitor! You are the reason we come," hisses Squamata.

"Who is a traitor?" the prince asks bravely.

"Dwarves! Dwarves plot to seize prince and kingdom. Lizardmen come to help," says Squamata.

"Dwarves? My guard? Impossible!" laughs the prince. "They are my sworn protectors."

At the lizardman's words, Sneed's band of dwarves bunch together with swords drawn.

"Sneed, what have you to say to these charges?" demands the prince.

"Sire, this is obviously a plot by the lizards to cast distrust upon dwarves, based on their own dislike of us. We must imprison them immediately to prevent whatever plot they have for taking over the kingdom."

A great hissing goes up from the thousands of reptilian throats.

"After all," continues Sneed in a calm voice, "they have no proof of their charges."

Urging the lizard chieftain forward, you leap off Squamata's back to the base of the throne and yell, "What about me, Sneed? Aren't I proof?"

"Who are you, brat? Should I know you?"

"You'd like to know me. You have patrols out searching for me. Where are my parents? If you've harmed them, you'll be sorry!"

Sneed's eyes flash with recognition and his face grows pale. Turning to the dwarf, the prince says, "Explain these charges, Sneed!"

"The child dreams, my prince. I know nothing of it or its parents."

The prince looks at you. "Speak now and explain your accusations. Fear not if you are right, but speak truly and weigh your words carefully." You need no further urging and repeat your story in a loud, clear voice.

At your words, Sneed and his dwarves band together. They begin to edge away, only to be surrounded by a wall of lizardmen. Seeing there is no escape, the dwarves hurl themselves on the lizardmen. Their swords strike the hard scales and bounce off. The lizardmen just brush away the blades.

Suddenly, Sneed draws a dagger and throws himself at the prince. His arm is raised to deliver a death blow as you rush forward and push the prince to safety. Seconds later,

Squamata's powerful arm crushes Sneed to helplessness.

"Why, Sneed? Why did you betray me?" asks the prince.

"All these years, mining, working, giving, and guarding what is rightfully ours. You may have won this time, but we dwarves will get even one day," snarls the captured Sneed.

"We shall see, Sneed," says the prince. "But somehow, I doubt it. I will make sure that you have no more chances to do anyone harm."

"Give dwarves to Squamata," hisses the giant lizard. "Lizardmen teach dwarves how to behave."

"I'll bet you would," laughs the prince.

Then, turning toward you, he becomes serious. "Galen, I owe my life to you. Would you and Sandy consider staying on here at the palace to become my counselors? This has proved that I need someone I can trust by me."

"Does that include Woofy?" asks Sandy.

"You bet," says the prince, laughing. "But first, more serious matters must be tended to. We must march against the dwarves and rescue your parents. Once the dwarves see Sneed in our hands, they will surrender!"

Certain of victory, you, Sandy and the lizardmen fall in behind the future king.

"You see, Sandy, it's just like I said—everything's going to be all right!"

THE END

As Woofy scrambles between your legs, you swing the rock down upon the dwarf's head. He collapses with a soft sigh.

"Good work!" cries a deep voice. "But hurry. A dwarf's head is hard. He'll soon be awake! Get the key out of his pouch and bring it here."

You do as you are bid and unlock the door.

The door crashes open, and an enormous, muscular dwarf stands before you.

The dwarf bends down and hugs the old king gently. "I knew you'd find a way to get me out of here, Father. Tell me what's happened."

"Sneed rides this very morning with all our warriors. He plans to kill the prince. Then he will have himself made king."

"There's no time to lose," says Bork. "We must leave immediately and hope we're in time."

"But what about my parents?" you ask.

"No time now. Are you with us or not?"

1) If you want to go with the dwarves and try to warn the prince, turn to page 106.

2) If you try to rescue your parents, turn to page 97.

3) If you want to try to stop Sneed here and now, turn to 149.

"Help! Help! Get me out of here. I'm down in the storm drain," you cry.

After a moment, an ugly dwarf face squints down at you.

"It's just some dumb kid and a dog. Got themselves stuck in a drain," says the dwarf, and soon the battle rages on again. You try to get someone to help, but no one listens. After a long time, all is silent.

You hear steps in the silence, then a bearded face peers through the grate. It's Sneed!

"Ah, there you are. I must admit, it's grand seeing you behind bars. I want you to know I'm going to do my best to keep things that way, now that I'm king."

THE END

It must be a very slow day for business at the palace. You wait for a long time, but no one comes and the door does not open.

Please turn back to page 145
and make another choice.

Clinging to Bork's cloak, you follow the dwarves through endless dark tunnels. At last you feel fresh air blowing on your face. Rolling aside a large boulder, the three of you creep out of the mountain.

You are standing in a narrow ravine filled with chomping and snorting horses.

"I'll take care of the guards, Galen," whispers Bork. "You two climb on a horse."

You choose a large black horse and somehow you and the old king climb on his back.

Bork returns on a long-legged white horse, holding a bridle. He fits the bit into your horse's mouth and tosses you the reins.

"Hope you can ride bareback. I couldn't take the time to find saddles."

Yelling loudly, he turns and races down the ravine. You follow close behind.

Sleeping horses waken and scatter before you. Yelling and screaming, the three of you pound down the path, stampeding horses through the open gates.

Suddenly, you hear another horse behind you. Glancing back, you see a dwarven guard riding hard to catch up.

You have two choices:

1) Swerve your horse and try to prevent the guard from following; turn to page 115.

2) Keep going and hope the guard will give up; turn to page 74.

As much as you want to, you cannot leave your mother in tears.

"Well, maybe it will be all right. Maybe the Boulderbenders will be able to warn the prince in time," you say with a sigh.

"It's not our fight, Galen. Don't get involved," says your mother.

"Maybe you're right," you say, and grasping your mother's hand, you lead her out into the dark corridor. After long hours of bumbling about in the dark, you find yourself outside, standing on top of the iron-red cliffs.

Below you, the dwarven army returns victorious.

Years later, as apprentice mapmaker to Sneed the Supreme, you wonder for the millionth time if you made a mistake in not going with Bork and Hume. If so, perhaps you will get a chance to correct that mistake. You have been contacted by Bork the Second, and you have agreed to help overthrow the evil Sneed. This time you will succeed.

THE END

"When will I meet your king?"

"Nearly there," answers Whimsy. "In fact, we're here. Turn toward me."

Whimsy places one small hand over your eyes and whispers softly. As she speaks, you forget what she is saying. Then she takes your hand and leads you to a hole in the base of an ancient tree. Down, down you go through a well-worn tunnel that spirals into the earth. When at last you stop, Whimsy mutters the magic words again.

"Where are we, Whimsy?" you ask, rubbing your eyes. "What happened? Did I go to sleep?" You open your eyes and blink with amazement.

You are in a large underground cavern. Above you, the roots of the forest poke through the earthen ceiling. They are covered with a shiny white fungus that lights the cave with a soft glow. Bright green cushion moss carpets the ground and large red and orange mushrooms dot its surface. In the distance, you can see a clear blue lake with small islands and many bridges.

"What does this mean, Whimsicality? Why have you broken the rule and brought a human into the secret caves? Explain yourself!" demands a gruff voice.

"Oh, Orff, don't be such a grump of a king. You know I wouldn't have done it if it weren't important. Besides, Galen won't remember anything. I cast a spell of forgetfulness before we came in."

"Spell or no, what can be so important that you would bring a human into our midst?"

"Great news! Great fun! That's what! The dwarves and that nasty Sneed are planning to kill the young prince and take over the humans' kingdom!"

"Great fun? What do you mean, great fun?" roars Orff. "This could mean our ruin! Disaster! After all the tricks we've played on them, they'll do their best to wipe us out. Especially Sneed. He's never forgiven us for the time he fell asleep in the forest and we carried him high up into that big tree and tied his beard around a branch. Remember how mad he was when he woke up and fell off? I've never heard such interesting curses in my whole life!

"And so you see, my dear young Whimsy, if they succeed in their plan, they'll chop down our forest and burn it to cinders. We've got to stop them!"

"Oh, goody! Great fun after all," laughs Whimsy, clapping her tiny hands gleefully. "Listen, everyone," she cries. "I've got this great plan. Let me tell you about it." And then all you can hear are whispers and giggles.

No one pays any attention to you, so you sit down next to Woofy and wait. After a long while, the pixies break their huddle and hurry away, giggling to themselves.

Finally, Orff approaches you. "Galen," he says, stroking his long blond beard, "we think we have a plan that will save the prince, the kingdom, and, of course, your parents. But the

plan will require your help if it is to work. Are you brave enough to help?"

"Tell me what I have to do," you say.

"The prince must be told of the danger so that he can muster the army," says Orff. "None of us can warn him. If he sees us, he'll think it's a trick, because the pixies have a reputation for . . . well, not being serious. It has to be you."

"But how can I reach the prince?"

"There are at least two ways," replies Orff.

1) "You can ride on your dog to the city and try to warn the prince." Turn to page 144.

2) "You can let us fly you in." Turn to page 75.

3) "Or, if you must, you can stay here and let us try to do it ourselves." Turn to page 58.

You stagger about on the sandy beach, your legs scarcely able to support you. Sandy rushes to your side, a burning branch in one hand.

"Thank the gods you're all right, Galen. I was certain that you would be killed."

"How did you escape?" you gasp.

"It's the fire. As soon as your yell woke me, I grabbed this stick. Lucky for me it was still burning. Snakes are afraid of fire, so I beat them off. But let's get out of here. They might get brave and come back."

Agreeing weakly, you cling to Sandy. The two of you make your way to the raft, watchful against another attack. Woofy cringes between your feet, his belly scraping the ground.

Sandy quickly launches the raft, and the three of you scramble on board. You watch the glowing campfire fade into the distance.

"Is it safe to travel at night, Galen?"

"I don't know, Sandy, but I'd rather take my chances with the river than with those snakes."

"I guess you're right," Sandy says glumly. "Well, I'll stand watch. This time, you sleep."

"I don't think I can sleep," you say. But battling the snake has worn you out, and the murmurings of the river soothe you into sleep.

A short time later you are wakened by what sounds like chewing.

"Sandy, do you hear anything?"

Sandy leans forward listening. "No. Do you?"

"I thought I did, but I don't hear it now. I guess it was my imagination," you say and you lie back on the wooden planks. But now Woofy is staring at the floor of the raft with his head cocked to one side. He seems to be listening.

The noise begins again. It IS chewing! As you stare at the raft, trying to figure out what the sound can be, the logs in front of you move.

A sleek head pops through the narrow opening. Red eyes glare at you.

"Sandy!" you screech. "HELP!"

As soon as you scream, small figures claw their way on board and scurry toward you. The raft is alive with wriggling, chittering, squeaking bodies. Red eyes and long, sharp teeth gleam in the dim glow of Sandy's torch.

"OH, NO! Swamp rats!" screams Sandy.

"What can we do?" you yell in terror.

Woofy's angry barking turns to terrified yelps and he scratches at your legs.

Quickly you scoop him up, kicking a rat at the same time.

"I don't know, but we'd better do it fast," cries Sandy, waving the remains of the torch.

1) "We can jump into the river and swim for it," you yell. If you choose this method, turn to page 73.

2) "I can try to scare them off with the torch," cries Sandy. If you choose this method, turn to page 66.

You yank the reins, turning the horse into the path of the oncoming rider. The plunging horses, screaming wildly, crash into each other with a tremendous impact. The guard's horse staggers and then falls heavily to the ground. The guard falls free. He struggles to remount, but the frightened horse scrambles to its feet and disappears into the mass of stampeding animals.

Your own horse manages to keep its footing. With a last look at the enraged guard, you turn and race away.

Please turn to page 45.

Using her tiny bow, Whimsy shoots several arrows, one after another, at the dwarves.

Both dwarves leap to their feet in bewilderment. Even after they pluck the tiny arrows out of their skin, they continue to stagger around as if they were drunk.

Laughing in bright bell tones, Whimsy flies down to within a few feet of the groggy dwarves. They stare at her stupidly, arms dangling loosely at their sides, mouths open.

"You two shouldn't be wandering around here by yourselves. You'll get eaten by wolves. Why don't you go home?"

The dwarves stare at her blankly.

"Go home!" she says, stamping her foot. "There, behind you. Those mountains! Turn around and start walking. Stay on the path and you won't get lost. Now go!" and she claps her hands sharply.

Staggering from side to side, the dwarves wander down the path in the general direction of the mountains.

You stare in amazement as the dwarves slowly walk away. "What did you do to them?"

"Oh, just a little trick I know," she says.

"Will they be all right?"

"Probably. If they stay on the path, someone will find them. But they won't remember us or what happened or anything else for that matter. So don't worry. Now come along, we've got plenty of ground to cover before dusk. If you keep on standing around like a giant statue, we'll never get there."

With one last look at the vanishing dwarves, you quickly follow Whimsy and Woofy in the opposite direction.

Soon you enter a dense forest. Thick moss carpets the ground and pale green ferns tower above your head. It is a strangely silent forest, and your voice sounds unnaturally loud when you ask Whimsy where you are going. She does not answer but just floats before you like a large brilliant butterfly.

Your path follows a route that no human feet ever made. Scrambling to keep up with Woofy and Whimsy, you cross bright brooks, climb big rocks and fallen trees, and stumble through forests of giant flowers. The sun, and even the sky, are lost in the crisscrossed tree branches high above you. You wonder if the pixie is trying to lose you.

At last, stumbling and tired, you fall in front of the largest oak tree you have ever seen. "Whimsy, I just can't go any farther right now. I must rest."

The pixie grins at you and settles lightly on a vine. Using the head of a dandelion, she powders her nose with lichen dust.

As you lie upon the ground watching her, a mist rises. At first you think that it is ordinary ground fog that appears in forests and swamps. But then you realize that it seems to be seeping out of the base of the large oak tree.

Sitting up quickly, you stare at the mist and rub your eyes. Maybe you're seeing things. No, it's still there. And now a figure seems to

be forming—the figure of a beautiful woman. The mist figure kneels, rests her chin in her hands and studies you carefully.

You are unable to take your gaze from the deep brown eyes that stare into your own. You are frozen by a powerful magic. Just as you feel that you must surely shatter into a million pieces, the pressure is released.

Tossing her long, thick, brown hair back over her tanned shoulders, the lovely creature turns to Whimsy and whispers softly, "What would you have me do this time, Whimsy? Turn the poor thing into a spider? I like the looks of this one. May I have it? I'll take good care of it. I won't lose it like I did the last one."

"No, Liana," says Whimsy. "For some reason, I've taken a fancy to this one, too. It needs my help. So long as it's fun, I think I'll keep it. Things have been really boring lately. Maybe this will stir things up a little. If it gets dull, I'll bring it back to you."

"Do you promise?" asks the dryad.

"You don't trust me?" fumes Whimsy.

"Of course not. We tree spirits weren't born yesterday, you know. Trusting a pixie is like trusting a cloud to go where you tell it to go. Now tell me what you want or I shall leave." Even as she speaks, her image begins to fade into the trunk of the tree.

"Wait! Don't go! We need your shrinking potion! The human's too large to go unnoticed in the forest! Please! I would be ever so grateful if you would."

The dryad's large brown eyes turn toward you once again. "What do you want, human? Would you like to go with me and see things few mortals have even dreamed of? Or would you like to get shrunk and go with someone you can barely see?"

1) If you want to be shrunk and go with Whimsy, turn to page 26.

2) If you would like to go with the dryad to see things no mortal has ever seen, turn to page 53.

3) If you would like to run away from these strange creatures, turn to page 122.

Holding Woofy in your arms, you lower your face until it nearly touches his. "Listen, Woofy, this is what I want you to do," and you whisper quietly in his ear.

Putting the puppy down, you cross your fingers and hope for the best.

As soon as the puppy's feet touch the ground, he dashes straight for the guard, yapping loudly and rushing in for quick nips with his tiny, sharp teeth.

Yelling with surprise and pain, the guard grabs his leg and swings his club at Woofy.

Woofy snarls and snaps at the guard's hand. The guard roars in rage and scrambles after Woofy, who is heading straight toward you.

You reach down and grab a large rock that lies at your feet . . .

Please turn to page 103.

Tearing your gaze away from the strange woman in the tree, you turn and run away as fast as you can.

"How dull," says Whimsy to the dryad. "This human looked as if it had promise, but I guess I was wrong."

"You should have given it to me," says the dryad. "I would have known how to use it wisely. You pixies are too hard on humans. Now, go away before I get really angry with you."

"Oh, nuts! I'm not afraid of you, you old tree stump," Whimsy says bravely. Nevertheless, she and Woofy back quickly into the forest, out of the reach of the angry dryad.

Deep in the forest, you continue to run, still frightened by your narrow escape.

At long last you stumble out of the enchanted forest. You are found by a group of travelers going to the city and join them in their cart. You try to tell them about the dwarves and the prince and the pixie, but they just laugh and think you are crazy. When you reach the city, everyone you tell the story to laughs and walks away. Soon, as the dwarven army rides into town, they stop laughing. But by then it is too late.

THE END

You go on shouting, "Nobody stole your land. The pact between Hume Boulderbender and the king was honorable, approved by the Council. What you should ask is how all who knew of it died. All but Sneed. You have been enslaved, not by the humans, but by Sneed. He sacrificed you to his own greed.

"Boulderbender, step forward," you command in a bold tone, hoping the old king is there.

"I'm here," quavers Boulderbender, "and I tell you all, too, that Sneed is your enemy, not the humans. It is time to live in peace."

"Let today be a day of new beginnings," says the prince. "Let us end our differences."

"The prince is right," cries a dwarf. "But Sneed should pay for his treachery."

"Wait!" squeaks a voice trying to sound commanding. "I can explain everything." But the mob roars and chases him down the street.

The street is silent above you. "Um, hello up there. Is anyone still there?"

A face appears. "So there you are. Hang on, we'll have you out in a flash."

Soon, you and Woofy stand in the town square, dripping and dirty, facing the prince.

"It looks like I have you to thank for my life," he says.

"And for giving us a chance to solve the problems facing our two kingdoms," adds Bork. "Once the true story is known, I'm sure that all will be well."

THE END

"Quick, Whimsy, do anything. But do it fast. I can scarcely breathe!" you groan.

Vaguely, through the ringing in your ears, you hear the now familiar POOF! In the blink of an eye, a flaming ball arcs through the air and streaks toward the golem.

It staggers backwards and crosses its huge arms in front of its face. You are still clutched in its grasp. "Whimsy, where are you?" you scream. "Are you all right?"

Woofy barks wildly. Whimsy does not answer.

At that moment the fist-sized ball of flame returns and zooms in tight circles around the monster's head. The golem opens its hands, dropping you to the ground.

You are stunned but alive. Scrambling to your feet, you and Woofy run into the forest. You hear no sound of pursuit, so you quickly hide behind a large tree and look for Whimsy. You don't see her.

The fireball moves around the creature like an angry bee, darting in and then zooming away before the giant hands can bat it away. Then the fireball begins to fly in ever-tightening circles around the creature's head. The golem shakes its head violently and rocks back and forth. But it cannot escape.

With a swooshing hiss, the fireball streaks in and lands atop the monster's head. Instantly, flames shoot up. Before your amazed eyes, they rapidly spread all over the wooden man. Thrashing about hysterically, the golem runs

into the woods. Long after it disappears, you can hear its frantic flight.

As you sigh with relief, the fireball appears before you. It floats in a lazy circle and comes to rest on your hand. Startled and frightened, you shake it off and turn to run. But you hear a familiar laugh, then, POOF! Whimsy stands before you. She reaches for the glowing fireball, and bounces it from one hand to the other. "TA DA! Did you like it? I thought it worked quite well."

She tosses the fireball to you and, without thinking, you catch it. "It's not hot!" you exclaim in wonder. "However did you do it?"

"Oh, it wasn't hard. It's just a little simple magic. It's not real fire. The golem just thought it was—like you did. I turned myself into a fire elemental—to make me look as if I were made of fire. It's simple if you know how. But wasn't it a great joke?" asks Whimsy, laughing and giggling.

"It's great, Whimsy. I'm really glad you can do stuff like that. But don't you think we should get out of here before the golem figures it out and comes back. It probably won't think it's so funny."

"Quite right," says Whimsy. "Golems don't have much of a sense of humor."

The two of you climb upon Woofy's back and slip into the dripping forest.

Please turn to page 109.

Pulling the horses into the trees at the edge of the road, you hide and wait until thundering hoofs and booming war drums announce Sneed's arrival.

"Open the gates!" roars Sneed.

"Go away! It's not time!" yells the guard.

"Open the gate or it will be past time for your head to rest on your neck," snarls Sneed.

There is a moment's silence, and then the guard says in a tiny voice, "Oh, maybe it is time after all. I think I see the sun coming up now." The large wooden gates creak open, and Sneed and his men thunder through into the sleeping city.

As soon as the last dwarf passes through the gates, the three of you mount your horses and follow them. The gate guard glowers down at you and mutters angrily to himself.

As you creep through the empty city streets, you hear the army roar, "Sneed! Sneed! Sneed! Long live Sneed the Supreme!"

Suddenly there is a clatter of hoofs and three horses dash by you. Tied to the saddle of one of the horses is a boy no older than yourself. A small crown rests crookedly on his head and tears streak his cheeks. For one short moment, the boy looks into your eyes—his look filled with despair—and then he is gone.

Just then, a small bent figure walks by the alley where you are hiding. He rubs his thin hands together and chuckles to himself. "At last, the king is dead, his son captured, soon to be in a dwarven cell, and those meddlesome Boulderbenders out of the way. Now all I have to do is let Sneed rule for a little while. When the time is right, I'll slip a poison mushroom into the stew. Then it's King Snively! No more 'Yes, sir. No, sir' ever again."

"Not if I can help it," you say, leaping out of the alley. Before Snively can say another word, you bang him on top of the head with a large rock and he falls to the ground with a thud. You drag him into the alley, search his pockets, and discover a large ring of keys.

"Bork, do you recognize these keys?"

"Of course. They're the keys to the dungeon cells," answers Bork.

"I thought he'd have them," you say. "Help me tie him up. I think we should ride back to the caves, rescue the prince and my parents from their prisons, and throw Snively into the deepest dungeon."

"It will also give me a chance to talk to my warriors. Once they know I am free, they will revolt. By morning Iron Mountain will be ours and your parents and the prince will be free and safe."

Happily, you turn and ride toward the caves in the mountains.

THE END

"Why should I believe you?" you demand. You turn and face the pixie.

"Because it's my forest. I live here and I know what's safe and what's not. Believe me, if I say that's a witch, that's a witch!"

"Okay, okay, I believe you. But I am tired, hungry, and cold."

"Well, I can take care of that. Why didn't you say something before this?"

Muttering under your breath, you follow the pixie as she carefully skirts the clearing. The little old lady hums pleasantly as she bastes the chicken. You feel a strong desire to join her in spite of the pixie's warning, but you keep walking.

Soon the witch is far behind you, and the pixie sighs with relief. "That was close! I was really scared. If you had gone, I don't know if I could have rescued you. Here, this is as safe as you'll ever get." Bending down, Whimsy digs into the mossy ground and pulls up a section of grass and earth. Beneath it is a dark tunnel.

Whimsy and Woofy disappear into the tunnel and even though you are nervous about it, you follow them. You have not taken more than two steps when the entrance closes behind you.

"I thought you said you were hungry," calls Whimsy. "Well, hurry up. Dinner's ready."

As you round a bend in the tunnel, you see an amazing sight. You are in a large round room. Its walls are covered with a soft white silky material that shimmers in the breeze of your movement. Whimsy sits down cross-legged in front of a number of bowls piled high with food which sends forth mouth-watering smells.

"Where did all of this come from?"

"I made it happen," says Whimsy. "It's one of the side benefits of being a pixie. But stop talking and eat."

An hour later, Whimsy waves her hands over the empty dishes and POOF!, they all disappear. "Much easier than washing them," says the pixie, noting your surprise. "Now we'd better get to sleep." With another gesture from Whimsy, the soft silky material arranges itself into beds, pillows, and blankets.

As you crawl into the soft bed, you ask sleepily, "What is this place anyhow?"

"It's a giant trap-door spider's den. I just borrowed it for the night."

All thoughts of sleep vanish from your mind as you sit up straight in the bed.

"A giant spider's den! What if it comes back?"

"Oh, don't be such a scaredy mouse. It won't be back. At least I don't think so."

1) If you trust Whimsy, lie down, and go to sleep. Turn to page 32.

2) If you don't want to have anything to do with a spider, turn to page 11.

You walk along the wall, patting it with your hands. "I know it's here somewhere," you mutter. "My father said it was." Woofy frisks ahead of you, and Bork follows behind, helping his father and looking puzzled.

Angry noises break out at the gate.

"Whatever it is you're doing, do it fast, Sneed's here," says Bork. "That fool of a guard will not prevent him from entering."

"I know it's here somewhere," you say, looking closely at the walls.

Just then Woofy begins to bark, but it's a curiously muffled sound.

"Here it is!" you cry and begin tearing at the ivy that clings to the stone. Plunging through the greenery, you find yourself in a cool, dim, brick-lined tunnel.

"What is this place?" growls Bork.

"It's an old storm drain. My dad told me about it. It might get us into the town."

"Well, let's get on with it," urges Bork. The three of you hurry into the dark, damp tunnel. Soon the walls and ceiling start to narrow. Then the tunnel ends completely at a solid brick wall. In its center, at waist height, is a hole, not a very big hole, with water dripping out of it.

"This is as far as we go," says Bork.

"What do you mean?" you cry. "We can't give up now. We've got to keep going or Sneed will kill the prince!"

"Use your eyes," snaps Bork impatiently. "We dwarves will never get through that pipe.

We're too big in the shoulders. If you want to continue, you're going to have to go by yourself. My father and I will go back to the gate. If Sneed has entered the city, no one will even notice two more dwarves. You and the dog get in there and do the best you can. Maybe one of us can make it and warn the prince."

Before you can answer, Bork picks you up and pushes you into the dark pipe, into the unknown.

You can see nothing. Water drips on you from above. Soon, you are very wet and very scared.

Ahead of you, you can hear Woofy barking as though urging you on. The sound echoes through the narrow space. Suddenly, the tunnel branches! New tunnels open to your left and right as well as continuing straight ahead.

From the left, you hear the sound of rapidly running water. To the right, you hear nothing at all, but there is a feeling of great space.

1) If you choose to go left, toward the sound of running water, turn to page 85.

2) If you choose to go right, turn to page 142.

3) If you decide to continue straight ahead, turn to page 55.

"I don't think I want to deal with those dwarves either. I'll be honest—they scare me, too. But I don't think they'll hurt my dad or mom, because my dad's valuable to them.

"It sure would be nice to have someone else around. Do you really have a boat?"

"Sure," says Sandy. "Well, it's really only a raft and I've never used it for anything but fishing, but I think it'll work just fine. C'mon. I'll show you."

Crossing the small clearing, Sandy enters the forest. You and Woofy follow close behind. The narrow path winds ever more deeply into the forest between trees of great age.

Soon you hear the sound of rushing water and, rounding a bend in the forest, you see the river stretching before you.

Broad and brown, it flows sluggishly between banks thick with rushes and cattails.

"Why's the water so dark?" you ask. "I thought rivers were blue or green."

"It's brown because it goes through swamps and mud flats upstream," answers Sandy.

"Looks creepy. Are there any swamps and mud flats downstream?"

"I don't know. I've never been any farther than the next mile or so," Sandy confesses.

"What! How are we going to get to the city if you don't even know if the river goes there?"

"It was your decision. I was just trying to help. If you want to change your mind, you can. But I really do think the river goes to the city eventually."

You stare glumly at the brown water. "I still think it's creepy," you mutter unhappily. "Anything could be in there and you wouldn't know it until it ate you."

"I'll admit there are some strange things in that water, but nothing's ever eaten me," says Sandy.

"Well, I guess I don't really have any choice. Let's get going. Where's the boat?"

"It's over here." Sandy parts the rushes and walks through water, which quickly rises over his ankles.

You pick up Woofy and follow Sandy nervously. The warm water sloshes about your legs, and soft sucking mud grasps at your feet.

"Here she is. Isn't she a beauty!" Sandy exclaims with pride.

Hurrying to his side, you part the reeds and look down at the most miserable raft ever built. Constructed of discarded boards and crooked logs of different sizes, all bound together with frayed and knotted cord, the raft floats heavily and unevenly in the water.

"Isn't it beautiful? I made it all by myself," says Sandy, pride shining in his voice.

"Is it safe?" you ask nervously.

"Of course, it's safe! I've been out in her lots of times," says Sandy. "Come on. Let's launch her!"

Carefully you place Woofy on the bobbing raft and help push it free of the reeds.

"Quick! Hop on!" cries Sandy. "This is the best part."

You nearly lose a boot to the thick bottom mud, but finally you wrench loose and heave yourself on board.

The current seizes the lumpy craft. First it swings left, then right, then it spins about in a tight circle.

"Didn't I tell you!" yells Sandy, his face flushed with excitement. "Isn't this fun!"

"It would be more fun if I knew that this thing wasn't going to come apart in the next five minutes," you say nervously as you cling to the rough planks.

"Don't worry," says Sandy, sitting down next to you. "I don't think it'll come apart. And anyway, it's smooth sailing from here on—at least for the next mile or two."

"Well, I guess we'll just have to hope for the best," you say with a sigh.

The sun rises high in the sky as the crude craft drifts along with the current. The gentle bobbing motion is very pleasant. You stretch out on the warm wood and watch the water flow by. Green banks dotted with bright, swaying flowers line both sides of the broad, brown river. Slowly you relax. You almost feel safe.

Just as you are about to fall asleep, Sandy whispers, "Wow! Look at that!"

Jerking upright, you stare in shock at an immense black scaly dragon stretched out on a chain of large rocks that crosses the river. The ugly head lies just short of the left bank. The monster's eyes are shut. Its long legs dangle into the water. Its tail washes back and forth in the current near the right bank.

"What is it?" you ask, not certain you believe your eyes.

"It's a black dragon," says Sandy. "Sometimes they'll swoop down and pick up a whole big sheep or cow and just fly away. They're really fierce. What are we going to do?"

1) "Maybe we should forget the whole thing and turn around and go back You can go back to the farm, and I can follow the dwarves." If this is your choice, turn to page 72.

2) "We could try to attack the dragon or at least scare it away." If this is your choice, turn to page 49.

3) "We could try to slip under the dragon between those two big rocks and hope it doesn't wake up." If this is your choice, turn to page 24.

4) "Or we could try to reach the right bank and carry the raft downstream around the dragon." If this is your choice, turn to page 141.

"We must try to stop Sneed and rescue the prince. But who are you? What's this all about?"

"My name is Hume Boulderbender and I was king of the Iron Mountain dwarves until I lost my throne through my own vanity.

"For many lifetimes we dwarves have mined the Iron Mountains for iron and precious gems. Ten years ago, it seemed we had taken all the mountain had to offer. We made plans to mine another mountain across the valley.

"But then an odd thing happened. The king of the humans visited us. He told me that his hobbies were geology and chemistry. While on a trip he had collected some samples from our mountain. Later, back in his laboratory, he experimented and discovered what he thought was a new metal. He asked if I would be interested in seeing the metal and arranging to mine it."

The old man sighs deeply, "I laughed at him. Who was he, a mere human, to tell dwarves there was treasure they had left unfound.

"When I refused him, he asked me to sell him the mineral rights to the mountain. He said he would mine it himself.

"The idea of a human mining seemed so funny that I persuaded my dwarven council to do as he asked. And so we sold him the mineral rights to the mountain for ever and ever. We laughed when he sent his army with picks and shovels. But we stopped laughing when they

brought out a mineral we had never seen before. When refined it made armor that was easy to fashion and of a finer quality than any we knew how to make.

"Things became worse. I could not break the contract, and all efforts to locate metal and gems in other mountains failed. It looked as though we would be forced to leave the place that had been our home for centuries. My people began to turn away at the sight of me. It was then that my eyesight began to fail. Sneed called it an omen and began his plot to overthrow my rule.

"Then the king made us an offer. If we would stay and mine the metal for him, one-fourth of it would be ours. We were also made the King's Guard, protecting the kingdom and the metal.

"Some thought it an honorable bargain and were happy to remain in their homes. Others, stirred by Sneed, said ALL metals belonged to dwarves and to settle for less was an insult. They said that I had sold their birthright and turned them into the slaves of men. In vain I reminded them that the council had ALL voted.

"When the king died—and some whisper that it was no accident—Sneed began saying that now, before the prince could be crowned, was the time for things to change. I woke one morning to find my son Bork imprisoned and Sneed leading my army.

"Not all agree with Sneed, but they fear him. Terrible things happen to those who oppose him. I am not afraid of him, but my eyesight has failed and I can do nothing to stop him without help."

"But what can I do?" you ask.

"You can help me free Bork. The army will follow him and maybe he can stop Sneed. Most dwarves have honor. They do not break their word or kill the sons of kings. Please, I beg of you, help me."

1) If you decide to help, turn to page 90.

2) If you decide it's too scary, ask the dwarf to show you the way out. Turn to page 17.

Kneeling, the two of you quickly work two poles from their bindings.

"Now, pole like mad for the right bank. With luck we can get out of the current."

The thick mud at the bottom of the river clings to your poles. But slowly you draw nearer to the bank and the great dragon tail.

At last the raft bumps to a halt. The immense scaly tail floats lazily in the water a mere foot away. You tug the heavy raft up onto the bank and into the thick green foliage.

"I didn't think we'd make it," you say between ragged breaths.

"Neither did I," gasps Sandy, "but we had to. That dragon would have eaten us for sure."

After you regain your breath, the two of you pull the raft through the deep grasses until you are safely past the sleeping dragon.

"This should be okay," wheezes Sandy. Quietly you ease the heavy raft into the water. It slips from your numb fingers and flops into the water with a loud splash. Both of you freeze with fear and hold your breath. The dragon's tail twitches restlessly, but the great beast does not stir from the sun-drenched rocks.

Scarcely breathing, you clutch Woofy and step aboard the raft. As you pole away, one large silver eye blinks open. The dragon heaves a deep sigh of relief as your raft rounds a bend in the river and passes from his sight.

Please turn to page 41.

You crawl hesitantly along the inside of the pipe. You cannot see anything, and you are becoming very nervous. Suddenly, sharp teeth nip your ankle and you are pulled backwards.

"Woofy, what are you doing? Let go. You're hurting me." Struggling to free yourself from the puppy's teeth, you slip and sprawl face down. "Now look what you've done. I'm all wet and dirty. Go away!"

You reach out to push yourself up, but you touch nothing. You feel about quickly, but your searching hand finds nothing but empty space. A cold chill wind blows upward out of the dark emptiness. Wedging yourself firmly in the narrow pipe, you sit huddled in a small heap and wait for your heart to stop pounding. A small warm body inches its way into your lap.

"Thanks, Woofy. If you hadn't stopped me, I'd probably still be falling."

You have two choices:

1) You can go back and turn to the left; turn to page 85.

2) You can go back and continue straight; turn to page 55.

You wriggle out from beneath the blankets and pick up the first heavy thing you find—a shovel.

Leaping from the seat of the wagon, you attack the nearest dwarf. Unfortunately, the shovel does little but annoy it. He picks you up, laughs loudly, and thumps you on the top of the head with a heavy fist.

Your mother screams, and everything goes black. Maybe you will recover and be able to help your parents escape later, but for now, it's . . .

THE END

Please go back to page 7
and begin another adventure.

Whimsy rides with you to the edge of the forest.

"You'll be fine. Just keep riding straight and you'll come to the city gates."

"I'm scared," you whisper.

"I know you are," says Whimsy, patting you on the shoulder. "But you have to do this even

if you are afraid because you're the only one who can talk to the prince. We're counting on you, and we won't be far behind."

You nod your understanding, square your shoulders, and turn and ride away.

"It's up to us now, Woofy. We have to do it!"

Woofy runs swiftly and soon the walls of the city rise before you. As you near the gates, you see a caravan of wagons and cows moving through them. You quickly direct Woofy into the milling mass to avoid being seen.

"What's that?" shouts a guard. "There! Among the cows! Stop that pixie! Stop that dog!"

But before the guards can stop you, Woofy darts into a side alley and you follow quickly.

You wander through narrow streets for a long time before you find your way to the foot of the palace steps. Two guards stand beside massive iron doors, their eyes staring straight ahead. The heavy doors are closed. How can you get in?

1) Sit and wait for someone to come and open the door; turn to page 105.

2) Talk one of the guards into letting you in; turn to page 16.

3) Try to find another way in; turn to page 148.

Ignoring the pixie's worried shouts, you run down the hill straight toward the dwarves, yelling, "Kidnap my parents, will you, you rotten dwarves? I'll show you." You pick up a handful of rocks and begin throwing them at the figures that crouch behind the boulders.

As you near the dwarves, one of them rises and throws a heavy club at you. It strikes you full on the forehead. A dull roar fills your ears and everything fades to gray . . . and then black.

One of the dwarves prods you with his toe. "Sneed will be glad we found this kid. Come on, Bulgar, let's get back. I'm hungry and I want to collect that reward."

The other dwarf grunts his agreement and heaves you over his broad shoulder. The two dwarves turn and trot away toward the distant mountains.

"Well, we can't help him now," says the pixie to the puppy. "Maybe we can rescue him later, but I don't think it's going to be easy." Sadly the two small figures watch as you disappear over the horizon.

Your fate is unknown, but for now you have reached . . .

THE END

You clutch your pole, prepared to die, when suddenly the current grabs the raft and whirls you away into the mist.

Before you can do more than hold on, you are dropping, falling like a rock over the edge of the waterfall. The mist is thick as a cloud. You can't see anything.

Abruptly, the raft slams to a stop. Water pounds down on you. You can feel logs strain, pull and break apart. Desperately you throw your arms around one and hold tight as you are swept once again out into the current. You are battered and half drowned, but you do not let go of the log. You do not know what has become of Sandy, but Woofy wriggles inside your shirt. At least he is alive.

Please turn to page 12.

Keeping out of sight of the guards, you edge along the wall of the palace. Windows are open above you, but they are too high to reach. Soon the wall curves into a garden where you see a small, slender boy playing alone.

Before you can stop him, Woofy rushes up to the boy and licks his face.

"Hi, pup!" says the boy warmly. "Where did you come from?" Then he spots you. "Who are you? If you're a pixie, you're not allowed here."

"No, I'm not a pixie," you say irritably. "I just got shrunk. It's only temporary. And I can't leave. There are about five trillion dwarves getting ready to attack and the pixies want to help and I've got to find the prince and tell him so that he can call out the army."

The boy stares at you in amazement, then says, "You can stop looking. I'm the prince."

"Gosh, I'm sorry! I didn't know," you say, dropping to one knee.

"Get up! Get up! I hate all that nonsense. Now, tell me what this is all about."

Quickly you tell the tale. Then the prince says, "I don't know why, but I believe you. I will alert the army. You get the pixies. Together we'll defeat the dwarves."

You clasp the prince's hand firmly, leap upon Woofy's back, and ride happily away. You are afraid of the coming battle, but you know the dwarves will be defeated and you'll see your parents soon.

THE END

"I think it's best to stop Sneed now, before he causes any serious mischief," says Bork. "It will be tricky, but it's the only way."

You shiver with fear, but, trying to be brave, you say "Count me in. I'll help if I can."

"Good! Now this is what I want you to do. Follow the path along the left side of the cavern. Inside every door that bears a black fire opal, you'll find a Boulderbender. Wake those within and tell them to gather their weapons and be ready at dawn.

"I will take the right side of the cavern, and my father will take the back. By dawn we will have gathered those who are loyal."

"But will they believe me?" you ask.

"Here, take my ring so they will know that your word is true and that it is not a trick."

Bork takes the ring from his finger and places it in your hands. Wrought of solid gold, the ring is heavy and large enough to hold three of your fingers. Centered in the middle of the coil of gold is a large oval fire opal. In the darkness the black stone disappears, making it seem that the fiery red flashes and starbursts of milky white float free in its midnight depths. You close your hand about the ring, feeling the heat of its radiance.

"I'll do my best, sir. And I'll keep the ring safe, too," you say.

"I know. That's why I trust you with this important mission. Go carefully and be safe."

Gripping the ring tightly, you climb the steep trail. You pass several houses before you come to one that has a fire opal implanted in the middle of its door.

Holding your breath, you grip the knob and push. All is darkness within. Carefully you creep forward until your outstretched fingers touch a sleeping figure. Instantly the figure leaps up. You hear the rasp of steel. A hand grabs your shirt, and the sharp, cold edge of a blade is pressed against your throat.

"Who meddles with Wolf Born in his own den?" growls a deep voice.

"Please don't kill me, sir. Bork sent me," you squeak fearfully.

"Bork, eh? Prove it!" hisses the dwarf.

You produce the ring with quivering fingers.

"By the gods, it is his!" exclaims the dwarf. He releases you and sheathes his blade.

"Old Wolf didn't scare you, did he? You can't trust anyone these days. Tell me, where did you get this ring and why do you come to Wolf in the night?"

Still clutching the ring, you tell the dwarf your message.

"Heh heh heh," chuckles Wolf. "Tell Bork he can count on me. Now get on with you. There are many more who will join this fight. We have feared Sneed for too long."

You leave Wolf to his preparations and step back onto the trail.

A neatly tended house built of glittering stones is the next to bear a fire opal. A small pool in the mossy lawn holds several blind cave fish, which swim in and out of the rocks.

Again you creep in slowly. Your hand finds a shoulder and gently you shake it. A terrified squeak comes out of the dark.

"Help, Daddy! It's a monster," screams a little voice.

"How many times do I have to tell you there are no monsters?" says a sleepy voice.

"Yes, there are! And one just grabbed me!" shrills the little creature under your hand.

"I'm no monster! Bork sent me," you whisper as an oil lamp flares up. A large, sleep-tousled dwarf and his wife, both dressed in long night gowns, squint at you from across the room.

"Bork? Is he free?" demands the dwarf. You show the ring and tell your tale.

"At last," sighs the dwarf.

"I told you there were monsters," squeaks the child, peeking from beneath its covers.

"It's not really a monster, dear. It's a human," says its mother. "They're not too pretty, but they won't hurt you."

"No. It's a monster," says the child, and he covers his head with the blankets.

"Oh, dear," clucks the mother. "Just when I had him convinced there were no such things, you had to come along and scare him."

Making apologies, you back out of the house and continue on up the path.

Throughout the long night you carry out your mission. You never lose your fear of waking the sleeping dwarves, but remembering your parents and the prince, you continue on.

Some waken ready to fight, others are thick with sleep, all are glad to hear your message.

As dawn tints the cave, you realize with relief that you have come to the end of the trail. There are no more houses. Looking down at the quiet cavern, you wish that it could stay this way. But inside the houses, dwarves are preparing for war and death.

You tuck yourself behind a boulder and wait. As you watch, a figure on the floor of the cave strikes a large, shiny disk and a loud BOOM! echoes forth. Once, twice, three times, five times, the gong fills the air.

Instantly, dwarves begin pouring out of their houses. Males pull on their armor, fix swords and war hammers to their belts. Females and children kiss and hug husbands and fathers good-bye. Some are crying.

Soon the trails are filled with dwarves heading for the cavern floor where they line up in rows.

Sneed, followed by Snively, strides back and forth in front of his army. He is talking, but you cannot hear the words. You would like to hear and see what is about to happen. You begin to edge down the trail.

You creep into one of the mossy gardens on a lower-level ledge and hide behind a concrete lawn statue. You press closer. Soon you will be able to hear everything.

But then the statue tilts, wobbles, and disappears over the ledge. You teeter on the edge of the crumbling ledge, trying to keep your balance. Arms waving wildly, you feel yourself slipping, slipping, slipping, and then falling through the air.

You land with a sickening thump. The world whirls about your head. Slowly, you raise up on your elbows, shake your head, and look around. Snively lies unconscious beneath you, and you are surrounded by frowning dwarves. Fear builds within you. A shadow falls over you. Looking up, you see Sneed. His sword is pointed at your heart.

"You certainly have a way of making your presence known," hisses Sneed. "I think you are about to meet with a terrible accident. Your parents will just have to learn to live with their loss. Say your prayers. You've meddled for the last time."

You close your eyes and throw your arm in front of your face as Sneed raises his sword.

You hear the clash of steel on steel and a gasp of shock.

Opening your eyes, you peek over your arm and see Sneed and Bork standing toe to toe with swords locked.

"No more killing, Sneed," says Bork. "Not this young person, not the prince, and not one dwarf."

"You're a dead dwarf, Boulderbender," hisses Sneed. "Seize him! Seize him at once!" he yells.

Several dwarves rush to do Sneed's bidding. Instantly, loyal Boulderbenders draw their swords. There is a brief flurry of fighting and suddenly it is over.

But Sneed keeps trying. "Fellow dwarves! Think of glory! Think of wealth! Think of the keys to the kingdom!" he screams. "Kill all Boulderbenders! Attack!"

Then Bork calls out, "Think of dying! Think of treachery! Think of deceit! The Boulderbenders have led you honorably for centuries. Don't throw that away for Sneed."

There is a tense moment, and then all of the dwarves begin to chant, "Boulderbender! Boulderbender! Boulderbender!" as they throw their weapons on the ground.

"None of you has vision," spits Sneed. "I was meant for glory. You don't deserve me!"

"Quite true, Sneed. We don't deserve you. I don't think anyone does," answers Bork. "Take him away and throw him in the deepest dungeon. Maybe he'll reform over the next century."

"How masterful, sir!" It's Snively, awake again. "May I commend you on how well you handled that situation, sir? The mark of a true leader. I always knew you'd escape and win the day, sir. And with me at your elbow, you cannot fail," says Snively. The little dwarf sports a large lump on his forehead.

"Guards! Take this one and throw him in with Sneed. They can keep each other company."

"No! No! Wait, sir! Don't do it, sir!" cries Snively as the guards drag him away. You stare after Snively and Sneed, who are yelling and screaming at each other as they are led away. Suddenly you are enfolded in softness.

"Galen, oh Galen. We were so afraid you'd been killed." It's your mother.

"We're very proud of you," says your father. "King Boulderbender has told me how brave you've been. I will make sure that the prince hears the entire story. He is a fine fellow, and I'm sure that he and the dwarves will be able to work out a new agreement that will be acceptable to all."

Just then Woofy climbs into your lap and begins to lick your face. Looking up, you see both Boulderbenders and your parents smiling at you. Beyond them are the hordes of cheering dwarves.

You give Woofy a thankful squeeze. You know you will all live happily ever after.

THE END

ENDLESS QUEST™ Books

Ask for these exciting DUNGEONS & DRAGONS™ titles at better bookstores and hobby shops everywhere!

#1 DUNGEON OF DREAD
You are a fighter in quest of treasure, willing to challenge the evil wizard in his mountain hideaway. Only by quick thinking and action will you emerge safely from the Dungeons of Dread.

#2 MOUNTAIN OF MIRRORS
An elven warrior hoping to keep your village from starving, you must enter the mysterious Mountain of Mirrors to fight monsters who have been stealing caravans of food.

#3 PILLARS OF PENTEGARN
You and your friends, Fox and Owl, journey into the ruins of Castle Pentegarn. You join three adventurers who are after the powerful Staff of Kings.

#4 RETURN TO BROOKMERE
You are an elven prince who must return to the ruins of the family castle, Brookmere, and learn what evil lurks there. Only courage and cleverness will bring you out.

#5 REVOLT OF THE DWARVES
The dwarves who once served your kingdom have revolted. You and your family are the first humans to be captured. But you escape! You must warn the prince and save your family.

#6 REVENGE OF THE RAINBOW DRAGONS
You are Jaimie, wizard apprentice to Pentegarn, on quest to Rainbow Castle to meet the challenge of three evil wizards. You must use wits and courage to save yourself.

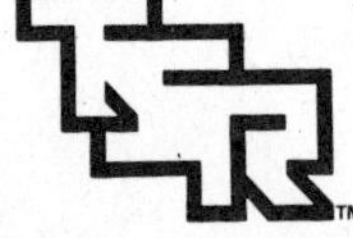

The Official Fuel for Over 100,000 of the World's Most Imaginative Gamers
• DRAGON™ Magazine is a storehouse of information.
It's the acknowledged leader. No other hobby gaming magazine has the size and circulation.
• DRAGON™ Magazine is actually a monthly role-playing aid.
It fuels the best players with ammunition from the best writers. Imaginative articles by the co-creator of DUNGEONS & DRAGONS® games, E. Gary Gygax, appear in each issue. Hundreds of authors and games from all manufacturers are featured throughout. And with a cost of only $24 for your year's supply of fuel, it's hard to imagine how you got anywhere without it!
For information write:
Subscription Department, Dragon Publishing
Box 110, C186EQB Lake Geneva, WI 53147
DRAGON™ Magazine
Box 110, C186EQB
Lake Geneva, WI 53147
In the UK:
TSR Hobbies, (UK) Ltd.
The Mill, Rathmore Rd.
Cambridge, ENGLAND
CB1 4AD
TSR Hobbies, Inc.
Products Of Your Imagination™
DRAGON is a trademark owned by TSR Hobbies, Inc. ©1983 TSR Hobbies, Inc. All Rights Reserved.